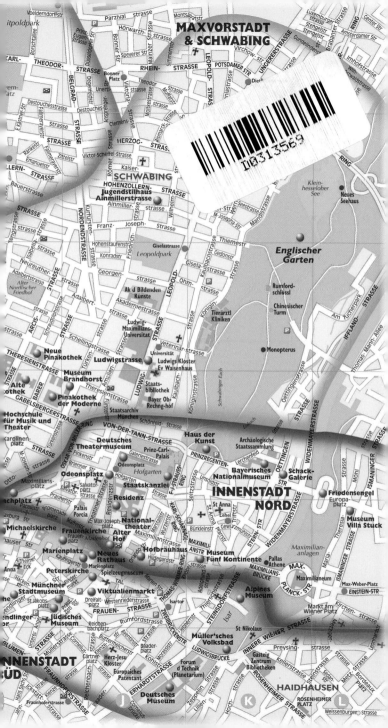

Contents

Introducing Munich

Munich has a unique atmosphere that is hard to define although many have tried: village of a million; metropolis with a heart; the secret capital of Germany. What is clear, is that this city has much more to offer than just beer and lederhosen.

With its big-city atmosphere, rural Alpine charm, art treasures, folk customs and high-tech industry, this cosmopolitan yet traditional metropolis manages to combine German urban efficiency with Southern European *joie de vivre*. According to a national survey, over half the German population, given the choice, would like to live here. As author Thomas Wolfe once remarked: "How can one speak of Munich but to say it is a kind of German heaven? Some people sleep and dream they are in paradise, but all over Germany people dream they have gone to Munich."

The city's close historic associations with the rise of Nazism cannot be ignored. However, we can be grateful that after World War II, although half its buildings were reduced to rubble, unlike so many German cities, Munich chose to restore and reconstruct the great palaces and churches of its past.

Many visitors are attracted to its handsome parks and palaces, its world-class museums, galleries and opera house. Others are drawn by the patriotism and deep-rooted conservatism of its inhabitants, who still cherish their age-old folk traditions. For lederhosen and felt hats with shaving-brush tufts are still worn, not to mention the dirndl-clad waitresses in the beer cellars clasping at least a dozen steins of lager. And, as you link arms with a stranger to sway to the music of an oom-pah band in one of the city's celebrated beer gardens, the atmosphere brings out the best in everyone: an infectious sociability, a love for outdoor pursuits and, above all, the Münchners' passion for life.

FACTS AND FIGURES

● Munich hosts the world's largest beer festival with its *Oktoberfest* and is home to six breweries.

● Munich has 1,200km (750 miles) of cycle paths and bikes represent 17 percent of the traffic.

● Bayern Munich is Germany's most successful soccer club with 27 league titles, 18 cup wins and eight European trophies.

MUNICH AND NAZISM

Munich will always be associated with Adolf Hitler. Indeed, he once remarked "Munich is the city closest to my heart. Here as a young man, as a soldier and as a politician I made my start." It was here, at the famous bloody Beer Hall Putsch of 1923 when he stormed a meeting of local dignitaries in the Bürgerbräukeller, that he made his first bid for power.

MYSTERY WIND

The famous *föhn* wind, Munich's unique weather phenomenon, can strike at any time of year. This warm, dry Alpine wind guarantees blue skies and crystal-clear views (the Alps seem close enough to touch) but it is also blamed for headaches and bad moods. So if bartenders seem more short-tempered and the locals more blunt than usual, perhaps it's the *föhn!*

MANN'S SHINING CITY

"München leuchtet" (Munich shone), the opening words of *Gladius Dei* (1902) by the celebrated German writer and Nobel Prize winner Thomas Mann, is without doubt one of Munich's most famous quotations. Today, Munich remains Mann's shining city. His words are on its medal of honor—"Munich shines—on Munich's friends."

A Short Stay in Munich

DAY 1

Morning Start the day with a traditional Bavarian breakfast of *Weisswürste* (boiled white sausages) at the **Schneider Bräuhaus** (▷ 42). A true Münchner enjoys them with a stein of beer!

Mid-morning Make your way to **Marienplatz** (▷ 28) in the Altstadt (old town). This is where the city's heart beats loudest. The square is dominated by its neo-Gothic town hall. Watch its Glockenspiel in action at 11am or midday, then climb 306 steps up the tower of nearby **Peterskirche** (▷ 31) for a brilliant view of the city.

Lunch Taste some local delicacies from various stands at the **Viktualienmarkt** (▷ 33), known for its vibrant market traders.

Afternoon Head to the **Kunstareal** (art district) where you can experience a remarkable two millennia of Western art in just a handful of museums and galleries.

Mid-afternoon Choose from the **Staatliche Antikensammlung** or the **Glyptothek** (both ▷ 67) for classical treasures; the **Alte Pinakothek** (▷ 63) for Old Master paintings; the **Neue Pinakothek** (▷ 69) for 18th-century and Impressionist art, and the **Pinakothek der Moderne** (▷ 70) for 20th- to 21st-century collections.

Dinner Return to the heart of the city for a substantial Bavarian meal in **Haxnbauer im Scholastikahaus** (▷ 58), an atmospheric old inn where chefs cook shanks of pork *(Schweinshax'n)* over open beechwood fires.

Evening Where better to spend your first evening in Munich than soaking up the atmosphere in the legendary **Hofbräuhaus** (▷ 47)?

DAY 2

Morning All the family will love the world-famous **Deutsches Museum** (▷ 24) with its fascinating hands-on science exhibits.

Mid-morning Shopaholics should enjoy souvenir shopping in the pedestrianized heart of the city. **Kaufingerstrasse** is the main shopping precinct, while **Theatinerstrasse** and **Maximilianstrasse** contain the city's most exclusive boutiques.

Lunch The tiny **Nürnberger Bratwurst Glöckl** (▷ 42) is popular with both locals and tourists alike, with its warm, friendly atmosphere and some of the best sausages in Munich, grilled over an open fire and served with mountains of sauerkraut on pewter plates.

Afternoon Head west to visit **Schloss Nymphenburg** (▷ 84), summer residence of the Wittelsbachs, and stroll in its magnificent grounds; or relax in the **Englischer Garten** (▷ 64), Munich's famous green lung, where locals go walking, jogging, busking, swimming and sunbathing.

Mid-afternoon Enjoy some refreshment at the **Chinese Tower** (▷ 65) beer garden, one of Germany's largest beer gardens, seating around 7,000 people.

Dinner Tuck into some traditional Bavarian fare at **Zum Franziskaner** (▷ 58), before crossing Max-Weber-Platz for an evening's operatic entertainment at the celebrated **Nationaltheater** (▷ 48, 57). If opera is not your style, there's sophisticated **Schumann's** (▷ 57) for cocktails.

Evening You'll find plenty of late-night bars and clubs in the **Gärtnerplatz** district, or head to fashionable **Schwabing** to see and be seen.

Top 25

► ► ►

Alte Pinakothek ▷ 62–63 One of the most important galleries in the world for Old Master paintings.

Viktualienmarkt ▷ 33 Bavaria's largest and best-known open-air food market.

Schloss Nymphenburg ▷ 84–85 One of Germany's largest baroque palaces and its grand park.

Schleissheim ▷ 100 Don't miss the masterpieces in the Great Gallery of the Neues Schloss.

Residenz ▷ 50–51 It is easy to imagine the Wittelsbachs' glorious heyday in the state rooms of this impressive palace.

Pinakothek der Moderne ▷ 70–71 One of the world's largest museums devoted to the visual arts.

Peterskirche ▷ 31 Munich's beloved ancient parish church has sweeping bird's-eye views across the city.

Olympiapark ▷ 82–83 Scene of the 1972 Olympic Games, this extensive park is hugely popular.

Asamkirche ▷ 26 A masterpiece of rococo architecture in the midst of a busy shopping street.

Bavaria Filmstadt ▷ 96–97 Glimpse behind the scenes of Europe's largest film studios.

Odeonsplatz ▷ 49 This city square is flanked by historic buildings and steeped in history and tradition.

Neue Pinakothek ▷ 69 The 19th- and 20th-century art and sculpture are a must for aficionados.

These pages are a quick guide to the Top 25, which are described in more detail later. Here they are listed alphabetically, and the tinted background shows which area they are in.

Map labels:
RIESENFELD
BMW Museum
Petuelpark
ALTE HEIDE
Nordfriedhof
Luitpoldpark
Hirschau
WEST SCHWABING
MAXVORSTADT & SCHWABING 59–78
SCHWABING
Leopoldpark
Englischer Garten
Alter Nordlischer Friedhof
Neue Pinakothek
Alte Pinakothek
Lenbachhaus
Pinakothek der Moderne
Königsplatz
Odeonsplatz
Hofgarten
Alter Botanical Garten
Residenz
National-theater
Bayerisches Nationalmuseum
BOGENHAUSEN
Frauenkirche
Neues Rathaus
Maximilian anlagen
LUDWIGS-VORST
Marienplatz
Peterskirche
Hofbräuhaus
Asamkirche
Viktualienmarkt
STEIN-HAUSEN
Jüdisches Museum
Münchner Stadtmuseum
Deutsches Museum
INNENSTADT NORD 43–58
HAIDHAUSEN
Alter Süd Friedhof
INNENSTADT SÜD 20–42
VORVORSTADT
Frühlings-anlagen
Ostfriedhof

◀ ◀ ◀

Shopping

Munich's most popular shopping street is without doubt the pedestrian zone between Karlsplatz and Marienplatz—one kilometer (half a mile) of shopping fun with huge department stores interspersed with boutiques and grocery stores. Even when the shops are closed this area is packed with window-shoppers. German fashions, leather and sportswear are all good buys. Just off Marienplatz, sports fans will revel in the giant sports department store SportScheck (▷ 39), where you can buy everything from golf tees to skiing holidays.

Munich Fashion
Munich is the capital of Germany's fashion industry, and you will be amazed at the city's enormous range of boutiques, from haute couture and Bavarian *Trachten* (folk costume) to wacky new trends. In the elegant shops of Theatinerstrasse, Residenzstrasse and Maximilianstrasse famous designer labels rub shoulders with the classic Munich boutique of Bogner Haus (▷ 55).

Waterproof Cloth
Be sure to visit Loden Frey (▷ 56), the largest shop for national costumes in the world—look for articles in Loden cloth, a Bavarian specialty. This waterproof wool fabric, in grey, navy or traditional green, has kept Münchners warm in winter for generations.

CULINARY DELIGHTS

Local culinary specialties include countless types of tasty sausage, best eaten with *Süßsenf* (sweet mustard), as well as aromatic regional herbs and fine breads and cheese, all magnificently displayed on green wooden stalls at the traditional open-air Viktualienmarkt (▷ 33), while Dallmayr (▷ 55) and Feinkost Käfer (▷ 55) are among the finest delicatessens in Europe. For truly unique chocolates, visit Elly Seidl (▷ 55), famous for its *Münchner Küppeln* chocolates, shaped like the onion-domes of the Frauenkirche.

Clockwise from top left: Tulips on Neuhauserstrasse; Shopping in Maximiliansplatz;

Publishing and Porcelain

As one of the world's leading publishing cities, with over 3,000 publishing houses, it is hardly surprising that Munich boasts a wide variety of bookshops, concentrated in the city's core and near the university in Schellingstrasse. Antiques shops, too, are popular, with many specializing in "English," Jugendstil (art nouveau) and art deco styles. Collectors keep a look out for old Meissen or modern Rosenthal, while the famous Nymphenburg porcelain (▷ 56, 90)—produced in Munich since 1747—is still manufactured in its traditional rococo designs. For the finest in Bavarian handicrafts, visit the Kunstgewerbeverein (▷ 56) in Pacellistrasse, or the numerous streets converging on Max-Joseph-Platz, for unique Bavarian gifts, including handmade puppets, carnival masks and porcelain beer steins.

Beer and Breweries

No shopping spree would be complete without purchasing some of Munich's beer. The main breweries are Spaten-Franziskaner, Augustiner, Löwenbräu, Hacker-Pschorr, Hofbräuhaus and Paulaner. There are special glasses for special beers, special beers for certain seasons—all making ideal gifts. And with beer halls every-where, it won't take long to find out if your preferred beer is a *dunkles*, *Weissbier*, *Pils* or *helles*… As they say in Munich, *Prost*!

SPECIALTY SHOPPING

Munich has a large number of small, old-fashioned shops that concentrate on one or two articles—for example, musical boxes, felt, buttons, knives, wood-carvings and even lederhosen—and which are still to be found in the middle of town. Some of the best buys in Munich include German-made binoculars, telescopes, kitchenware, electronic gadgets and bed linen. The presence of so many top orchestras in Germany results in top-notch musical instruments. Germany is also known for its manufacture of children's toys. You'll find everything from train sets and teddy bears to traditional dolls and handmade puppets.

a Nutcracker doll stall at the Christmas Market; Munich's open-air Viktualienmarkt (above)

Shopping by Theme

Whether you're looking for a department store, a quirky boutique, or something in between, you'll find it all in Munich. On this page shops are listed by theme. For a more detailed write-up, see the individual listings in Munich by Area.

Antiques
Antike Uhren Eder (▷ 55)

Books
Deutsches Museum Shop (▷ 38)
Hugendubel (▷ 38)
Words' Worth (▷ 74)

Children
Kinder-Ambiente (▷ 74)
Kunst und Spiel (▷ 74)
Obletter (▷ 39)

Department Stores and Shopping Centers
Galeria Kaufhof (▷ 38)
Karstadt (▷ 90)
Ludwig Beck (▷ 39)
Olympia Einkaufszentrum (OEZ, ▷ 90)
SportScheck (▷ 39)

Fashion and Accessories
Bogner Haus (▷ 55)
Bree (▷ 55)
Ed. Meier (▷ 55)
Fourth Dimension (▷ 38)
Hemmerle (▷ 55)

Food and Markets
L'Antipasto (▷ 90)
Dallmayr (▷ 55)
Eilles (▷ 90)
Elisabethmarkt (▷ 74)
Elly Seidl (▷ 55)
Espresso & Barista (▷ 90)
Feinkost Käfer (▷ 55)
Markt am Wiener Platz (▷ 56)
Schmidt (▷ 39)
Spanisches Fruchthaus (▷ 39)
Viktualienmarkt (▷ 33, 39)

Gifts and Bavarian Souvenirs
Geschenke Kaiser (▷ 38)
Holz Leute (▷ 38)
Kunstgewerbeverein (▷ 56)
Lederhosen Wagner (▷ 38)
Loden Frey (▷ 56)
Max Krug (▷ 39)
Porzellan Manufaktur Nymphenburg (▷ 56, 90)

Rosenthal (▷ 56)
Weihnachtsmarkt (▷ panel 39)

Interior Design and Art
Deco Susanne Klein (▷ 38)
Kremer Pigmente (▷ 74)
Kristina Sack (▷ 90)

Specialist shops
China's World (▷ 74)
Fanshop (▷ 55)
Kaut-Bullinger (▷ 38)
Perlenmarkt (▷ 74)
Schreibmayr (▷ 56)

ESSENTIAL MUNICH SHOPPING BY THEME

Munich by Night

Munich's nightlife is relatively small-scale and provincial compared to some cities. On a mild summer's evening, nothing beats strolling through the old town, seeing the illuminated historic buildings, or pausing to enjoy a drink or an ice cream on the broad sidewalk terraces of Leopoldstrasse.

Eating and Drinking

Eating and drinking in Munich are major pastimes, with options ranging from hearty Bavarian fare washed down with massive liter-steins of beer in the local Bierkellers to some of Germany's finest restaurants. In both beer cellars and beer gardens, it is normal to sit together with other guests at long communal tables.

City of Music

Munich is a city of music, with a famous opera-house long associated with Mozart, Wagner and Richard Strauss, and three major symphony orchestras. The *Münchner Opern Festspiele* festival in July and August marks the musical highpoint of the year, attracting top international singers and opera aficionados. There's always something musical happening, from choral works and organ recitals in churches to open-air concerts at royal palaces, and live jazz, blues and rock events, not to mention marionette-opera performances and even yodeling. If your German is good enough, Munich also offers a dazzling schedule of first-rate theater, ranging from classical and contemporary productions to political cabaret.

From top: Fun and beer-drinking at the Oktoberfest; Cuvilliés-Theater in the Residenz

NIGHTSPOTS

Early-closing laws prevent many places from staying open all night, but Munich has plenty of vibrant bars and clubs, many on Gärtnerplatz, the student district of Schwabing and the Glockenbach quarter. Choose from foaming beer steins and drunken swaying to the oom-pah bands of the beer halls or sophisticated cocktails in Germany's most fashionable nightspots.

Where to Eat

Bavarian food, usually accompanied by a beer, is hearty and heavy and is almost always based on meat. White sausages, dumplings, sauerkraut and roast pork are just a few examples of local cuisine. Beer halls *(Brauhäuser)* are the best places to try traditional German food and sample some of the city's own beers.

Italian Connection

Munich has a strong affinity with Italy, which means the city has plenty of Italian restaurants. Locals share the Italians' love of dining alfresco —at the first hint of sunshine, chairs and tables are swiftly moved outside to terraces, courtyards and gardens. In recent years, the number of Thai, Japanese, Mexican and tapas restaurants in the city has also grown.

When to Eat

In Munich, people like to eat early and it is not unusual to find older Munich residents having lunch as early as 11.15am. As hotel breakfast buffets are substantial, you may not be hungry enough for an early lunch. In this case, choose one of the many bars, cafés and restaurants that serve full meals or even breakfast right into the afternoon. Another alternative for lunch is to head to Viktualienmarkt (▷ 33) with its casual food stalls. In the evening, those restaurants that aren't open all day start serving at about 6pm. Smoking is banned in bars, cafés and restaurants, including tents at *Oktoberfest*.

BÄCKEREIEN AND *KAFFEE UND KUCHEN*

Bakeries *(Bäckereien)* are usually the first eateries to open in the morning. They serve an overwhelming array of cakes, pastries, breads and coffees at very reasonable prices. Many bakeries have a small seating or standing area, so you can eat your purchases there. Cafés in Germany also often open as early as 7 or 8am, and tend to serve a wide range of light snacks, in addition to *Kaffee und Kuchen* (coffee and cakes), which are usually enjoyed mid-morning or late in the afternoon.

From top: Café Glockenspiel; a Munich beer garden; a street café in Neumarkt; traditional Würste

Where to Eat by Cuisine

There are places to eat to suit all tastes and budgets in Munich. On this page they are listed by cuisine. For a more detailed description of each restaurant, see Munich by Area.

Afternoon Tea
Schlosscafé im
Palmenhaus (▷ 92)

Bavarian Cuisine
Augustiner Gaststätten
(▷ 41)
Bachmaier Hofbräu
(▷ 77)
Halali (▷ 58)
Haxnbauer im
Scholastikahaus
(▷ 58)
Hofbräuhaus (▷ 47)
Löwenbräukeller (▷ 92)
Nürnberger Bratwurst
Glöckl (▷ 42)
Ratskeller (▷ 42)
Schlemmermeyer (▷ 42)
Schneider Bräuhaus
(▷ 42)
Welser Kuche (▷ 58)
Zum Alten Markt (▷ 42)
Zum Franziskaner (▷ 58)

Beer Gardens
Augustiner-Keller (▷ 92)
Kloster Andechs (▷ 102)
Max Emanuel Bräuerei
(▷ 78)
Seehaus im Englischen
Garten (▷ 78)
Waldwirtschaft
Grosshesselohe
(▷ 102)
Zum Flaucher (▷ 102)

Cafés
Café Altschwabing
(▷ 77)
Café am Beethovenplatz
(▷ 91)
Café Frischhut (▷ 41)
Café Glockenspiel
(▷ 40)
Café Joon (▷ 77)
Café Luitpold (▷ 58)
Café Reitschule (▷ 77)
Café Ruffini (▷ 92)
Schelling Salon (▷ 78)
Tresznjewski (▷ 78)

Gourmet
Bogenhauser Hof (▷ 58)
Einstein (▷ 41)
Kunstlerhaus (▷ 41)
Tantris (▷ 78)

Ice cream
Adamello (▷ 41)
Sarcletti (▷ 92)

International Cuisine
Call Soul (▷ 76)
Lemar (▷ 77)
The Potting Shed (▷ 78)
Romans (▷ 92)
Seoul (▷ 78)
Vinaiolo (▷ 42)
Waldfee (▷ 78)

Snacks
Dallmayr (▷ 55)
Elisabethmarkt (▷ 74)
Münchner Suppenküche
(▷ 41)
Viktualienmarkt (▷ 33)

Vegetarian
Café Ignaz (▷ 77)
Prinz Myshkin (▷ 42)

Top Tips For...

These great suggestions will help you tailor your ideal visit to Munich, no matter how you choose to spend your time. Each entry has a fuller write-up elsewhere in the book.

EXPLORING ON A SHOE-STRING

Visit Munich's churches for free, including lofty Frauenkirche (▷ 27), sumptuous Asamkirche (▷ 26) and beautiful Theatinerkirche (▷ 49).

Window-shop on glamorous Maximilianstrasse, with its glitzy designer boutiques.

Climb the Olympiaturm (▷ 82–83) for stunning views of the city and its Alpine backdrop.

While away an afternoon people-watching in the Englischer Garten (▷ 64–65).

CHILDREN'S ACTIVITIES

Star in a movie at the Bavaria Filmstadt (▷ 96–97).

Enjoy a dazzling performance at Munich's internationally acclaimed Circus Krone (▷ 91).

Marvel at science at the Deutsches Museum (▷ 24–25).

Visit the world's first Geo-Zoo (▷ 102).

STAYING IN LUXURY

Check into Munich's top hotel, the Kempinski Vier Jahreszeiten (▷ 112).

Be pampered at Le Meridien's spa (▷ 112).

Enjoy the top-notch restaurant at the majestic Königshof hotel (▷ 112).

Cosset yourself in the stylish surroundings of Bayerischer Hof (▷ 112).

LOCAL DELICACIES

Order the best *Weisswürste* in town at the Schneider Bräuhaus (▷ 42).

Try some *Leberkäs* (meat loaf), or *Bratwurst* with sweet mustard, from one of the stands at the Viktualienmarkt (▷ 33).

Tuck into a gigantic pork shank (*Schweinshax'n*) at Haxnbauer im Scholastikahaus (▷ 58).

Indulge in a sugary Bavarian *Kaiserschmarm* with apple puree at Augustiner Gaststätten (▷ 41).

Clockwise from top left: he Olympic Tower; an evening of jazz; enjoying stein of beer;

LIVE MUSIC

Chill out at the city's celebrated nightspot Jazzclub Unterfahrt (▷ 57).

Enjoy a concert in the splendid Herkulessaal in the Residenz (▷ 57).

Assess the future of German classical music at a concert or recital in the Hochschule für Musik (▷ 72).

DRINKING BEER

Try the Bavarian beer at the legendary Hofbräuhaus (▷ 47), complete with traditional music and servers dressed in folk costume.

See and be seen at the Augustiner-Keller beer garden (▷ 92).

Relax at the Chinesischer Turm beer garden in the Englischer Garten (▷ 64–65).

Enjoy live jazz at the atmospheric Grosshesselohe beer garden (▷ 102).

CONTEMPORARY ARCHITECTURE

Visit the world-class Allianz Arena football (soccer) stadium (▷ 101).

Notice how BMW's towering HQ (▷ 87) resembles a four-leaf clover.

See a symbol of modern Munich: Olympiapark's futuristic tent-roof (▷ 82–83).

Admire the 21st-century Herz-Jesu-Kirche (▷ 87), which boasts the world's largest church doors.

Explore the Jüdisches Museum and community center, whose buildings are a metaphor for the Temple of Solomon (▷ 32).

SHOPPING FOR BAVARIAN SOUVENIRS

Try on some *Trachten* (Bavarian folk costume) at Loden Frey (▷ 56).

Taste *glühwein* and delicious gingerbread while shopping at the annual *Weihnachtsmarkt* on Marienplatz (▷ panel, 39).

Shop for the fine pewter ornaments and objects that make unusual and attractive gifts at Geschenke Kaiser (▷ 38).

Classy Nymphenburg Porcelain is on sale at the Palace workshops (▷ 90).

Herz-Jesu-Kirche; the Christmas Market; a traditional meal; the 4D Cinema Experience

BIRD'S-EYE CITY VIEWS

Dine in the revolving restaurant atop the Olympiaturm (▷ 82–83), with its breathtaking views of the city and the Alps.

Climb the steps of Peterskirche's tower (▷ 31) for the best bird's-eye views of the city.

Look down on Marienplatz from the Neues Rathaus (▷ 28–29) viewing tower.

Climb one of the celebrated onion domes atop the Frauenkirche (▷ 27) for 360-degree views of the city.

EATING BRUNCH

Join the discerning crowd for pancakes and freshly squeezed juices at Joon (▷ 77).

Enjoy a sunny breakfast on the terrace of Café Reitschule (▷ 77).

Try trendy Café Altschwabing for a traditional Bavarian brunch (▷ 77).

Opt for the traditional Bavarian *Weisswurst* sausage breakfast from among the meat and cheese platters in Tresznjewski (▷ 78).

STYLISH DRINKS

Rub shoulders with models and celebrities at Schumann's (▷ 57), Munich's most sophisticated and fashionable bar.

Take your pick at sleek P1 (▷ 57) in the Haus der Kunst, which offers Munich's beautiful people a choice of eight bars to suit all tastes and moods.

Enjoy exotic cocktails at Master's Home (▷ 40), a long-standing favorite with Münchners.

BEAUTIFUL CHURCHES

Marvel at the lavish interior and religious treasures of the Asamkirche (▷ 26).

Admire the lofty Michaelskirche (▷ 35), the largest Renaissance church north of the Alps.

Hear the bells chime at Peterskirche (▷ 31), the city's oldest parish church.

Seek out the Devil's footprint inside Munich's Frauenkirche cathedral (▷ 27).

Look out for the Italianate features in the magnificent baroque Theatinerkirche (▷ 49).

From top: Frauenkirche; freshly squeezed juices; cocktails; Peterskirche and the maypole

Munich by Area

The city center is where Munich's heart beats loudest. From Marienplatz, the main square, it's just a stone's throw to the city's cathedral, the robust daily market and the main pedestrian shopping precinct.

Innenstadt Süd

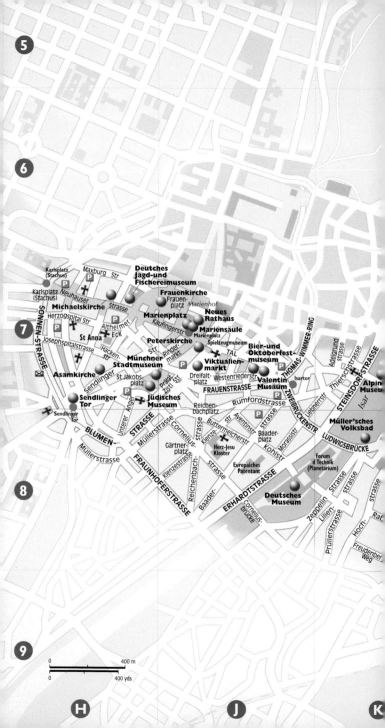

5

6

7

8

9

Karlsplatz
(Stachus)

Maxburg Str

**Deutches
Jagd-und
Fischereimuseum**

Karlsplatz
(Stachus)

Neuhauser

Frauenkirche

Frauen-
platz

Marienhof

SONNEN-STRASSE

Michaelskirche

Strasse

Marienplatz

**Neues
Rathaus**

Herzogspital str

Althelmer

Kaufingerstr

Mariensäule

St Anna

Eck

Marienplatz

Josephspitalstrasse

Hacken-
str

Peterskirche

Str

Rindermarkt

Spielzeugmuseum

**Bier-und
Oktoberfest-
museum**

**Münchner
Stadtmuseum**

**Viktualien-
markt**

TAL

THOMAS- WIMMER-RING

Adelgrund
strasse

Thierschstrasse

STEINSDORFSTRASSE

Asamkirche

Sendlinger

St Jakobs-
platz

Graggenauerstr
Zisel

Dreifalt-
platz

Westenriederstr

**Valentin
Museum**

Isartor

ZWEIBRÜCKENSTR

Liebherrstr

Isar

**Alpin
Museum**

**Sendlinger
Tor**

Unterer Anger

**Jüdisches
Museum**

FRAUENSTRASSE

Rumfordstrasse

**Müller'sches
Volksbad**

Sendlinger
Tor

STRASSE

Müllerstrasse

Cornelius

Reichenbach-
strasse

Buttermelcherstr

Aventinstr

Baaderplatz

Morassist

LUDWIGSBRÜCKE

BLUMEN-

Müllerstrasse

Klenze-
str

Baader-
platz

Kohlstr

FRAUNHOFERSTRASSE

Gärtnerplatz

Klenzestrasse

Herz-Jesu
Kloster

Europaiches
Patentant

Reichenbach
strasse

ERHARDTSTRASSE

**Deutsches
Museum**

Baader-
strasse

Zeppelin

Lilien-
strasse

Forum
d Technik
(Planetarium)

Prüllerstrasse

Hoch-

strasse

Rat

Cornelius-
brücke

Freudenber
Weg

0   400 m

0   400 yds

H   **J**   **K**

Maximilian-
anlagen

Nikolaus

INERE WIENER STRASSE

Preysing-   strasse

Gasteig
Zentrum
ibliotheken

Kellerstrasse

Steinstrasse

Sedan

Metzger- strasse

Strasse

Strasse Bordeaux
Platz

Leonhardstr

Kirchenstrasse

Hypopark

Solchenstr

Elsasser Strasse

STRASSE

HAIDHAUSEN

Metz-   strasse

Strasse

Belfortstr

OSTBAHNHOF

ROSENHEIMER
PLATZ

ROSENHEIMER-STRASSE

BALAN- STRASSE

FRANZISKANER- STRASSE

strasse

Weissenburger

Lothringerstrasse

Breisacher Cravelottestr

Strasse

Orlean's

Orlean's
platz

Ostbahnhof

Strasse

Mühldorfstrasse

Haager

str

P

Berufsb
zentrum

Frieden-

Grafinger

Strasse

Sieboldstr

Jugendwohnheim

Salesianum

Auerfeldstrasse

ORLEANS-

BALAN- STRASSE

ROSENHEIMER STRASSE

Bayerische
Volkssternwarte

P

Sankt

Cajetan- str

ANZINGER STRASSE

L   M

Deutsches Museum

HIGHLIGHTS

- Planetarium
- Karl Benz's Automobil Nummer I
- Copy of the Puffing Billy steam train
- Reconstruction of the Caves of Lascaux
- Dornier Do 31 and Junkers Ju 52 aircraft
- 19th-century sailing ship—60m (197ft) long

TIP

- The museum shop (▷ 38) is a great source for science books, souvenirs and quality museum-endorsed gifts to appeal to all ages.

If you spent one minute at each exhibit, it would take you 36 days to see everything at this museum of superlatives—Munich's most famous and Germany's most visited science museum.

Voyage of discovery In 1903, engineer Oskar von Miller founded the Museum of Masterworks of Science and Technology. After his death, the collection moved to its own island on the Isar, in the east of the city, and was officially opened in 1925. Over the years this giant technological playground has grown to a staggering 17,000-plus exhibits, ranging from the sundial to the space shuttle.

Learning experience The most popular areas cover man and his environment, computer

The Deutsches Museum sits on its own island on the Isar and houses one of the world's greatest collections of scientific and technological exhibits

science and various transportation sections. Alongside original objects are audiovisual displays, experiments and hands-on models.

Unique exhibits Some of the most dramatic displays are the star shows at the Planetarium (which take place in the high-tech Forum), an ear-splitting high-voltage demonstration that simulates a 220,000-volt flash of lightning, and the vast model railway on the ground level. Other highlights are a reconstruction of the caves at Lascaux; the first German U-boat (submarine); one of the first jet planes; Karl Benz's first car; the bench on which Otto Hahn proved the splitting of the atom and the fun, hands-on Kid's Kingdom area. The exhibits constantly evolve to reflect the latest historical and technological discoveries.

THE BASICS

deutschesmuseum.de

➕ J8

✉ Museumsinsel 1

☎ 217 9333

🕐 Daily 9–5

🍴 Restaurant, café

🚇 S-Bahn Isartor, U-Bahn Fraunhoferstrasse

🚌 131; tram 8

♿ Excellent

💶 Moderate

Asamkirche

TOP 25

The church of St. John Nepomuk is known as Asamkirche after its architects

THE BASICS

✚ H7
✉ Sendlinger Strasse 32
☎ 2368 7989
🕐 Daily 9–5
🚇 U-Bahn Sendlinger Tor
🚌 152; tram 17, 18, 27
♿ Free

HIGHLIGHTS

● *Gnadenstuhl (Throne of Mercy)*, E.Q. Asam
● Ceiling fresco, C.D. Asam
● Two-tiered high altar
● Wax effigy of St. John Nepomuk
● Statues of John the Baptist and St. John the Evangelist
● Portraits of the Asam brothers
● Facade

The Asamkirche may be Munich's finest rococo structure. A narrow but sensational facade provides a mere hint of the sumptuous interior—one of the most lavish works of the celebrated Asam brothers.

The Asam brothers In 1729, master architect and sculptor Egid Quirin Asam acquired a house in Sendlinger Strasse and built his own private church next door, assisted by his brother, a distinguished fresco artist. For this reason, the Church of St. John Nepomuk (a Bohemian saint popular in 18th-century Bavaria) is better known as the Asamkirche. Even though Asam financed the construction, he was forced to open it to the public, and the church was consecrated in 1746. Free from the normal constraints of a patron's demands, the brothers created a dazzling jewel of rococo architecture.

Lavish decoration The unobtrusive marble facade has an unusual plinth of unhewn rocks and a kneeling figure of St. John Nepomuk. The tiny, dark but opulent interior is crammed with sculptures, murals and gold leaf, and crowned by a magnificent ceiling fresco depicting the life of the saint. The long, narrow nave carries your eye to the glorious two-tiered high altar and shrine of St. John Nepomuk. The gallery altar, portraying the Trinity and illuminated by an oval window representing the sun, is crowned by Egid Quirin's *Throne of Mercy*, depicting Christ crucified, in the arms of God.

The twin towers of Frauenkirche are the symbol of Munich

Frauenkirche

This massive, late-Gothic brick church symbolizes Munich more than any other building. Its sturdy twin towers (99m/325ft and 100m/328ft high), with their Italian-Renaissance onion domes, dominate the city's skyline.

Munich's cathedral The Frauenkirche, built between 1468 and 1488, has been the cathedral of Southern Bavaria since 1821. Today's structure, the largest reconstructed medieval building in Munich, has been rebuilt from the rubble of World War II. Little remains of the original except the basic architectural elements and the windows in the choir. Its strength lies in its simplicity and grand proportions.

Onion domes Thirty years after the church's consecration, the towers were still roofless. In 1524, unique green Italian-Renaissance onion domes were erected as a temporary measure. With this eccentric addition to the structure, the building once provoked an irreverent comparison to a pair of beer mugs with lids. The domes became so popular that they were retained.

The Devil's footprint A footprint is visible in the stone floor by the entrance. Legend has it that the Devil stamped his foot in delight because the architect had apparently forgotten to put in windows, though the building was flooded with light. But Jörg von Halsbach's ingenious design meant that no windows were visible from this point, giving him the last laugh.

THE BASICS

+ J7
- Frauenplatz 1
- 290 0820
- Daily 7.30am–8pm
- U- or S-Bahn Marienplatz
- 52, 131, 152; tram 19
- None
- Free

HIGHLIGHTS

● Gothic stained-glass windows
● The Baptism of Christ, Friedrich Pacher altarpiece
● Jan Polack altar panels
● St. Lantpert's Chapel with wood figures of apostles and prophets from the workshop of Erasmus Grasser

Marienplatz and Neues Rathaus

HIGHLIGHTS

- Glockenspiel
- Facade
- Tower
- Ratskeller (▷ 42)

TIP

- Don't miss Konrad Knoll's famous Fish Fountain here, on the site of a former fish market. They say if you wash your purse here on Ash Wednesday, it will never be empty. The Lord Mayor still washes the City Purse here every year.

Eleven o'clock is the magic hour for tourists who crowd Marienplatz to see the world-famous Munich Glockenspiel in action on the lavish neo-Gothic facade of the New Town Hall.

Towers and turrets Marienplatz is the city's main square, and traditionally the scene of tournaments, festivals and ceremonies. It is also a great place to people-watch. The entire north side of the square is dominated by the imposing Neues Rathaus (New Town Hall), seat of the city government for nearly a century. Constructed between 1867 and 1909 around six courtyards with towers, sculptures and gargoyles, its neo-Gothic style was controversial at the time, but it has since become one of Munich's best-known landmarks.

Marienplatz, with the famous Glockenspiel on the Neues Rathaus (New Town Hall), is the heart of the city

The Glockenspiel On the main front of the building, figures of Bavarian royalty stand alongside saints and characters from local folklore. The central tower viewing platform offers a fantastic view of the city, and houses one of the largest Glockenspiels (carillons) in Europe. This mechanical clock plays four different tunes on 43 bells while 32 almost life-size carved figures present scenes from Munich's history—among them the jousting match at the marriage of Duke Wilhelm V with Renate of Lorraine in 1568, and the *Schäfflertanz* (Coopers' dance) of 1517, celebrating the end of the Black Death. This dance is re-enacted in Munich's streets every seven years (next in 2019). The Glockenspiel can be seen in action daily at 11am and also at noon and at 5pm in summer. The cuckoo at the end always raises a smile.

THE BASICS

+ J7
- Marienplatz
- 23 300 (Neues Rathaus)
- Tower: Mon–Sat 9–6
- Ratskeller beer hall and restaurant
- U- or S-Bahn Marienplatz
- 52, 131, 152
- Few
- Tower: inexpensive

Münchner Stadtmuseum

The City Museum is housed in the former armory

THE BASICS

stadtmuseum-online.de

✚ H7

✉ St.-Jakobs-Platz 1

☎ 233 22370

🕙 Tue–Sun 10–6

🍴 Café and beer garden

🚇 U-Bahn Sendlinger Tor, U- or S-Bahn Marienplatz

🚌 52, 62

♿ Good

🎟 Moderate

❓ Tours, lectures

HIGHLIGHTS

● History of the City section
● Marionette Theater Collection and fairground museum
● Photography and Film Museum

Munich's unique, lively, eclectic personality is reflected in the diverse nature of the City Museum's collections, which range from weapons, armor and fashion to fairgrounds, Biedermeier and films.

City history If your itinerary does not allow enough time to explore all the old parts of the city on foot, head straight to the History of the City section housed on the first floor, to study Munich's development since the Middle Ages through maps, models and before-and-after photographs, which illustrate the devastating effects of World War II bombing.

Unusual collections As the museum is housed in the former city armory, it is only fitting that it should contain one of the largest collections of ancient weaponry in Germany. Other collections worth visiting include fashion from the 18th century to the present day, the second-largest musical instrument collection in Europe and the Photography and Film Museum, with its fascinating display of cameras and photographs. Don't miss the greatest treasure—Erasmus Grasser's 10 Moriske Dancers (1480), originally carved for the Old Town Hall.

For children of all ages The Marionette Theater Collection (Münchner Marionetten-theater), one of the world's largest, reflects Bavaria's role in the production of glove-puppets, shadow plays and mechanical toys.

Known affectionately as Alter Peter, the city's oldest parish church is immortalized in a traditional song that claims "Until Old Peter's tower falls down, we'll have a good life in Munich town."

Built over time The Peterskirche dates from the foundations of the city itself in 1158, on a slight hill called the Petersbergl, where the monks (who gave their name to Munich) had established a settlement in the 11th century. The original Romanesque structure was expanded in Gothic style and renovated.

Destruction and rebirth During World War II the church was almost entirely destroyed. In an attempt to raise money to rebuild it, Bavarian Radio stirred the hearts of the people of Munich by playing only a shortened version of the "Alter Peter" song, and public donations flowed in. After the tower was completed, in October 1951, the full version was at last heard again.

Bells and a view The most extraordinary feature is the tower, with its lantern-dome and eight asymmetrically placed clock-faces, designed so that, according to Karl Valentin (▷ 35), eight people can tell the time at once. The chimes are renowned and the best time to hear them is at 3pm on Saturday, when they ring in the Sabbath. The 306-step climb to the viewing platform is rewarded by a dramatic bird's-eye view of Munich.

THE BASICS

➕ J7

✉ Petersplatz

☎ 260 4828

🕐 Tower Mon–Fri 9–6.30, Sat–Sun & holidays 10–6.30 (closes 1hr earlier in winter). Closed in bad weather

🚇 U- or S-Bahn Marienplatz

🚌 52, 131, 152

♿ None

🎫 Tower: inexpensive

HIGHLIGHTS

● High Altar (Nikolaus Stuber, Egid Quirin Asam and Erasmus Grasser)
● Clock tower
● Schrenk Altar
● Jan Polack's five Gothic pictures
● Mariahilf Altar (Ignaz Günther)
● Corpus-Christi Altar (Ignaz Günther)
● Aresinger-Epitaph (Erasmus Grasser)

INNENSTADT SÜD TOP 25

Jüdisches Museum

TOP 25

Door of the Ten Commandments; the New Synagogue and Judisches Museum

THE BASICS

juedisches-museum-muenchen.de

✚ H7

✉ St.-Jakobs-Platz 16

☎ 2339 6096

🕐 Tue–Sun 10–6

🍴 Cafe Exponat

🚇 U- or S-Bahn Marienplatz, U-Bahn Sendlinger Tor

🚌 62

♿ Very good

💰 Inexpensive

❓ Library: free. Ask for a "reader's badge" at the information counter. A Jewish Museum ticket stub gives 50 percent off admission to some other museums for 48 hrs.

HIGHLIGHTS

● Large interactive map of Munich with pictures and tales of Jewish families
● 19th-century embroidered satin Torah cover
● Glass-and-steel mesh filigree decoration on the New Synagogue
● Jordan B. Gorfinkel's (Gorf) cartoon *Everything's Relative*

At the heart of this built-for-purpose cultural center serving the city's growing Jewish community is a small but engaging museum showcasing local Jewish history, religion and modern life.

The permanent exhibition This traces Jewish history in Munich from the early 13th century. Eye-catching displays explain the significance of religious festivals such as Rosh Hashanah (New Year), Yom Kippur (Day of Atonement), Hanukkah (Festival of Lights) and Pesach (Passover), as well as rituals of life (circumcision, Bar Mitzvah, marriage and death).

Temporary exhibitions Thought-provoking temporary exhibitions of photography, art and installations by contemporary Jewish artists are enhanced by online study areas where visitors can discover more about the displays. The museum is a center for research and holds regular discussions and presentations on aspects of Jewish life. The extensive library, which is open to all, has a section for genealogical research.

Community center The terrace of the Café Exponat is the best place to take in the architectural concept: a metaphor for the Temple of Solomon. The buildings, comprising the New Synagogue, community center and museum, were designed by Rena Wandel-Hoefer and Wolfgang Lorch. Do not miss the comic strip silk-screen panels on the entrance by Gorf.

Viktualienmarkt

Less than a stone's throw from the cosmopolitan shops of Munich's main pedestrian zone, this bustling open-air food market, with taverns and cooked food stands, has retained its traditional atmosphere for centuries.

A long tradition In 1807 it was decided that the market in Marienplatz had become too small for the rapidly growing trade. So a new Viktualienmarkt was planned for a grassy field outside the city, where livestock grazed and stagecoaches stopped. Today it is Munich's oldest, largest and most attractive market, with its green wooden stalls and striped umbrellas.

Atmosphere The lively atmosphere of the market owes much to the robust market women, famous for the loud and lively abuse they dish out in earthy Bavarian dialect to their customers. Their goods are superb, the prices high and the variety of fresh produce is vast, ranging from Bavarian blue cheese to Alpine herbs and flowers. Look out for neatly tied bundles of asparagus in spring, and mountains of fresh cranberries in summer.

Open-air restaurant Try some Bavarian specialties from the little taverns and stands around the market—*Leberkäs* (meat loaf) or a *Brat-* or *Weisswurst* (fried or white sausage)—wash it down with a typically Bavarian *Weissbier* in the beer garden set up round the maypole, the scene of lively May Day celebrations.

THE BASICS

viktualienmarkt-muenchen.de

🚩 J7

🕐 Core hours Mon–Fri 10–6, Sat 10–3

🍴 Numerous stands serve hot and cold snacks

🚇 U- or S-Bahn Marienplatz

🚌 52, 131, 152

HIGHLIGHTS

● Irene Schwarz—more than 40 kinds of potato
● Exoten Müller—freshly pressed fruit juices
● Rottler—herbs, mustards, preserves and chutneys
● Münchner Suppenküche— soup kitchen (▷ 41)
● Nordsee—fish snacks
● Pferdemetzgerei Wörle—specialty sausages (including horsemeat sausages, so do check)
● Ludwig Freisinger—herbs and spices
● Honighäusl—herbal honey wines

More to See

ALPINES MUSEUM

alpenverein.de/kulturmuseum

This museum has everything you want to know about mountaineering in the Alps from 1760 onwards.

➕ K7 ✉ Praterinsel 5 ☎ 211 2240 ⏰ Tue–Fri 1–6, Sat, Sun 11–6 🚇 U-Bahn Lehel, U- or S-Bahn Isartor 🚋 Tram 17 💵 Moderate

BAYERISCHE VOLKSSTERNWARTE

sternwarte-muenchen.de

The Bavarian Observatory is fascinating, and a special late-night treat for children and parents alike.

➕ L9 ✉ Rosenheimer Strasse 145 ☎ 40 62 39 ⏰ Apr–Aug Mon–Fri 9pm–11pm; Sep–Mar Mon–Fri 8pm–10pm 🚇 U-Bahn Karl-Preis-Platz (Exit B) 💵 Moderate ❓ English show Mon 8pm Sep–Mar, 9pm Apr–Aug

BIER- UND OKTOBERFEST-MUSEUM

bier-und-oktoberfestmuseum.de

With its six breweries, Munich is the world's top beer metropolis. Housed in the city's oldest townhouse, this museum is devoted to beer and the *Oktoberfest*. Learn about the history of beer and why Munich's is so special.

➕ J7 ✉ Sterneckerstrasse 2 ☎ 2423 1607 ⏰ Tue–Sat 1–6 🚇 U- or S-Bahn Isartor 💵 Moderate

DEUTSCHES JAGD- UND FISCHEREIMUSEUM

jagd-fischerei-museum.de

The German Hunting and Fishing Museum has the most important collection of its kind in Germany. Don't miss the Wolpertinger, a hoax animal resembling a marmot with webbed feet, antlers and wings. Follow the Forest Trail *(Waldpfad)* for a multimedia exhibition.

➕ H7 ✉ Neuhauserstrasse 2 ☎ 22 05 22 ⏰ Daily 9.30–5 (Thu until 9) 🚇 U- or S-Bahn Marienplatz 💵 Moderate

MARIENSÄULE

Marienplatz owes its name to the gracious figure of the Virgin Mary on the column erected in 1638.

A boar guards the entrance to the German Hunting and Fishing Museum

The Mariensäule and the Neues Rathaus

All distances in Bavaria are measured from this column.

J7 ✉ Marienplatz 🚇 U- or S-Bahn Marienplatz

MICHAELSKIRCHE

st-michael-muenchen.de

The Jesuit Church of St. Michael was built at the end of the 16th century by Duke Wilhelm (the Pious) as a monument to the Counter-Reformation. Disaster struck in 1590 when the tower collapsed; it was finally consecrated in 1597. War damage has been masterfully repaired. Marvel at the Renaissance hall with its ornate roof.

H7 ✉ Neuhauserstrasse 6 ☎ 231 7060 🕐 Mon–Sat 10–7, Sun 7am–10.15pm 🚇 U- or S-Bahn Karlsplatz 🚋 Tram 16, 17, 18, 19, 20, 21, 27 💶 Free

MÜLLER'SCHES VOLKSBAD

Germany's loveliest indoor swimming pool, in the Jugendstil style.

K8 ✉ Rosenheimer Strasse 1 ☎ 2361 5050 🕐 Daily 7.30am–11pm 🚇 S-Bahn Isartor 🚋 Tram 18

SENDLINGER TOR

The medieval Sendlinger Tor town gate has a large central arch and two hexagonal flanking towers. It was once the southern exit through the town walls.

H7 🚇 U-Bahn Sendlinger Tor

VALENTIN MUSÄUM

valentin-musaeum.de

A fine showcase for the eccentric and distinctive humor of Munich's Karl Valentin (1882–1948), Bavaria's answer to Charlie Chaplin, much-loved for his quirky wit and misanthropic humor. He started out by entertaining the crowds in beer halls but soon attracted the attention of Schwabing intellectuals and is perhaps best remembered for his sketch in which he put fish in a bird-cage and birds in an aquarium. The museum contains various oddities, and has bizarre opening times.

J7 ✉ Tal 50 ☎ 22 32 66 🕐 Mon, Tue, 11.01–5.29; Fri, Sat 11.01–5.59; Sun 10.01–5.29 🚇 S-Bahn Isartor 💶 Free ❓ Contact the museum for tours in English

Müller'sches Volksbad–a Jugendstil public bath

Munich's Old Town

Explore the pedestrian heart of Munich, between its medieval west and east gates, taking in the cathedral, main square and market.

DISTANCE: 2km (1.2 miles) **ALLOW:** 2 hours (excluding visits)

KARLSPLATZ
✚ H7 🚉 S- and U-Bahn Karlsplatz

KARLSPLATZ
✚ H7 🚉 S- and U-Bahn Karlsplatz

❶ Pass through Karlstor, site of the former medieval west gate to the city, into Neuhauserstrasse, the main pedestrian shopping zone. Don't miss the Michaelskirche (▷ 35) on the left.

❽ Head back along Tal toward Marienplatz. Just before entering the square, look for the Old Town Hall, which also houses a toy museum. Cross Marienplatz, continue up Neuhauserstrasse back to the start point.

INNENSTADT SÜD WALK

❷ Turn left on Augustenstrasse to Frauenkirche (▷ 27), the cathedral, with its distinctive onion-shape domes. Return to the main shopping area via Liebfrauenstrasse and on to Marienplatz (▷ 28–29).

❼ Turn right into Westenrieder Strasse then first left up Sterneckerstrasse past the Bier- und Oktoberfest-Museum (▷ 34). Continue on to Tal. Turn right toward Isartor, Munich's most easterly remaining medieval gate. Inside one tower is the museum devoted to Karl Valentin (▷ 35).

❸ Head up Rindermarkt (beside Hugendubel bookshop, ▷ 38) to the Peterskirche (▷ 31). If you're feeling energetic, climb the tower—the view of the city is worth the effort.

❻ You will come to Gärtnerplatz, site of the celebrated Staatstheater (▷ 40). Proceed past the bars and restaurants of Klenzestrasse, cross Rumfordstrasse and Frauen Strasse until you reach Zwinger Strasse.

❹ Swing round the side of the church to the Viktualienmarkt (▷ 33), for some light refreshment in the beer garden or from one of the small food stands there.

❺ Cross to the far side of the market and continue down Reichenbachstrasse.

Shopping

DECO SUSANNE KLEIN

It's worth seeking out this tiny boutique near Gärtnerplatz if you are after state-of-the-art interior design, featuring colorful fabrics, curtains, cushions, classy pottery and more.

➕ J8 ✉ Klenzestrasse 41 ☎ 272 2427
🚇 U-Bahn Fraunhoferstrasse 🚌 52, 152

DEUTSCHES MUSEUM SHOP

deutsches-museum-shop.de
An amazingly diverse shop full of books, toys, puzzles and models based on the scientific and technical world, for scientifically minded children and adults. The perfect place to pick up an interesting present.

➕ J8 ✉ Museumsinsel 1 ☎ 2138 3892
🚇 S-Bahn Isartor 🚌 Tram 18

FOURTH DIMENSION

fourthdimension.de
Visit one of Germany's leading costume and design jewelry shops and you will be enchanted with the exquisite selection of earrings, necklaces and bracelets.

➕ J7 ✉ Frauenplatz 14 ☎ 2280 1090
🚇 S-Bahn Marienplatz

GALERIA KAUFHOF

galeria-kaufhof.de
Right in the center of town, this large department store is not only a handy stand-by for gifts, toys, perfumes and clothing, it also has an excellent wine and gourmet section.

➕ J7 ✉ Kaufingerstrasse 1–5 ☎ 23 18 51
🚇 U- or S-Bahn Marienplatz

GESCHENKE KAISER

geschenke-kaiser.de
This gift and souvenir store is one of Munich's oldest (founded in 1874). It has an enchanting and eclectic selection of pewter miniatures, cuckoo clocks, crib figures, beer jugs, candlesticks and much else besides.

➕ J7 ✉ Rindermarkt 1 ☎ 26 45 09
🚇 U- or S-Bahn Marienplatz

HOLZ LEUTE

holz-leute.de
Everything here is crafted from wood. Much of it is custom made in local workshops, so expect to pay a little more for originality. They sell everything from pepper pots and biscuit cutters to chess sets.

➕ J7 ✉ Viktualienmarkt 2 ☎ 26 82 48
🚇 U- or S-Bahn Marienplatz

HUGENDUBEL

hugendubel.de
This enormous bookstore is spread over four floors. There are even sofas where you can sit and read to your heart's content without buying! There are several more branches in the city.

➕ J7 ✉ Marienplatz 22 ☎ 3075 7575
🚇 U- or S-Bahn Marienplatz

KAUT-BULLINGER

kaut-bullinger.de
For a retro look in the computer age, shop here on three floors for chic stationery ranging from pens, writing paper and art materials to leather personal organizers and designer wrapping paper.

➕ J7 ✉ Rosenstrasse 8 ☎ 23 80 00
🚇 U- or S-Bahn Marienplatz

LEDERHOSEN WAGNER

lederhosen-wagner.de
This traditional shop has been making Bavaria's distinctive leather shorts from soft deerskin since 1825. Surprise your friends with a shaving-brush hat, made out of chamois hair, to match the shorts.

➕ J7 ✉ Tal 2 ☎ 22 56 97 🚇 U- or S-Bahn Marienplatz

LUDWIG BECK

ludwigbeck.com

Beck is without doubt Munich's most stylish department store. At Christmas artisans work on the top floor and the store becomes a wonderland of crafts.
🔲 J7 ✉ Theatinerstrasse 14 ☎ 23 69 10
📍 U- or S-Bahn Marienplatz

MAX KRUG

max-krug.com

Here is a useful port of call if you can't find that special gift or souvenir. Old Bavaria lives on in this treasure trove of traditional crafts and knick-knacks—handmade wooden cuckoo clocks, beer steins, nutcrackers, music boxes and more.
🔲 H7 ✉ Neuhauserstrasse 2 ☎ 22 45 01
📍 U- or S-Bahn Karlsplatz

OBLETTER

obletter.de

A traditional and comprehensive toy store where you will find everything from model trains to wooden toys, puppets, board games and cuddly bears.
🔲 H7 ✉ Karlsplatz 11–12 ☎ 5508 9510
📍 U- or S-Bahn Karlsplatz

SCHMIDT

lebkuchen-schmidt.com

Shop here for some of the best Nuremberg *Lebkuchen* (delicious gingerbread), also honey, Stollen (traditional festive fruitcakes) and other delicacies. Purchases are artfully packaged in parcels and collectable tins.
🔲 J7 ✉ Westenriederstrasse 6 ☎ 2323 8980 📍 S-Bahn Isartor

SPANISCHES FRUCHTHAUS

spanisches-fruchthaus.de

In the hands of the Schmöller family since 1912, this small shop has mouthwatering displays of fruits—dried and candied, crystallized or chocolate coated. It also sells delicious nuts and Spanish wines.
🔲 J7 ✉ Rindermarkt 10 ☎ 26 45 70
📍 U- or S-Bahn Marienplatz

SPORTSCHECK

sportscheck.de

A department store for sports fanatics, with six floors dedicated to every recreational activity imaginable. It's just an hour by car to the nearest ski slopes, and the store will even arrange day-long ski trips to the mountains.
🔲 H7 ✉ Neuhauser Strasse 21 ☎ 21660
📍 U- or S-Bahn Karlsplatz

VIKTUALIENMARKT

viktualienmarkt-muenchen.de

The largest and most famous Bavarian open-air food market (▷ 33). Look for the Kräuter-Freisinger stand which sells herbs and the Honighäusl stand for honey products. There are plenty of opportunities to try beer and food too. It's worth visiting for the atmosphere and bustle alone.
🔲 J7 ✉ Core hours Mon–Fri 10–6, Sat 10–3
📍 U or S-Bahn Marienplatz

WEIHNACHTSMARKT

Every Advent, Marienplatz comes alive with the magic of Christmas, with one of Germany's finest Christmas markets, and the air is filled with the aroma of *Glühwein* and roasted chestnuts. A spectacular 30m (100ft) Christmas tree is erected in the middle of the square, and surrounded by tiny wooden huts selling traditional crafts, toys, candles and Christmas decorations: look out for festive Nutcracker dolls, pretty hand-carved crib sets and delicious *Lebkuchen* (gingerbread) hearts.

Entertainment and Nightlife

CAFÉ GLOCKENSPIEL

cafe-glockenspiel.de

Named for Marienplatz's famous carillon (▷ 28–29) the café is popular for its roof terrace and cocktails. During the daytime the 1970s-style Espresso bar and café serves reasonably priced breakfasts and snacks.

➕ J7 ✉ Marienplatz 28 (5th floor) ☎ 26 42 56 🕙 10am–1am 🚇 U- or S-Bahn Marienplatz

GASTEIG

gasteig.de

Dating from the 1980s, this is the city's main cultural hub and is home to both the Munich Philharmonic Orchestra and the Conservatory. The concert hall has excellent acoustics. The center offers a rich program of events (see online for details) and there is a self-service restaurant.

➕ K8 ✉ Rosenheimer Strasse 5 ☎ 48 09 80 🚇 S-Bahn Rosenheimer Platz

HAVANA CLUB

havanaclub-muenchen.de

There are over 100 types of rum on sale, including genuine Cuban varieties, at this intimate bar. It's decorated in rich Spanish colonial style, with pictures of Ernest Hemingway on the walls.

➕ J7 ✉ Herrnstrasse 30 ☎ 29 18 84 🕙 Mon–Thu 6pm–1am, Fri–Sat 6pm–3am, Sun 7pm–1am 🚇 S-Bahn Isartor

HOLY HOME

A small bar with dim lighting valued by locals for the intimate atmosphere and reasonably priced draft beers. The music is as eclectic as the decor. It tends to get crowded on weekends.

➕ J8 ✉ Reichenbachstrasse 21 ☎ 201 4546 🕙 Daily 7pm–2am (Fri–Sat til 3am) 🚇 U-Bahn Fraunhoferstrasse 🚌 152

MASTER'S HOME

mastershome-muenchen.de

An extraordinary underground bar in the colonial style of an African farmhouse. You can choose between sitting in "the bathroom," "the living room" or "the dining room" (restaurant) or join the guests at the bar, which is cooled by a giant aeroplane propeller, and eat, dance or simply lap up the atmosphere over a delicious cocktail.

➕ J7 ✉ Frauenstrasse 11 ☎ 22 99 09 🕙 Daily 6pm–2am 🚇 S-Bahn Isartor

MÜNCHNER FILMMUSEUM

stadtmuseum-online.de/filmmu.htm

Join the eclectic crowd of cinema buffs in this small 165-seater auditorium for screenings (Tuesday–Sunday) from Germany's largest collection of silent movies.

➕ H7 ✉ St.-Jakobs-Platz 1 ☎ 2332 2370 🚇 U-Bahn Sendlinger Tor, U- or S-Bahn Marienplatz

MUSEUM LICHTSPIELE

movietown.eu

A former music hall that screens Hollywood blockbusters and cult classics in the original languages. The atmosphere is cozier here than in a typical multiplex.

➕ K8 ✉ Lilienstrasse 2 ☎ 48 24 03 🚇 S-Bahn Rosenheimer Platz 🚊 Tram 27

STAATSTHEATER AM GÄRTNERPLATZ

staatstheater-am-gaertnerplatz.de

Dating back to the 1860s, this flourishing theater claims to be the only municipal light opera house in the world, with a wide repertoire of operetta, light opera, musicals and ballet.

➕ J8 ✉ Gärtnerplatz 3 ☎ 20 24 11 🚇 U-Bahn Fraunhoferstrasse 🚌 52, 56

Where to Eat

PRICES

Prices are approximate, based on a
3-course meal for one person.

€€€ over €50
€€ €25–€50
€ under €25

kosher dining with a contemporary
flare. Vegetarian alternatives to the
meat and fish dishes are on offer in
every instance.

H7 St-Jakobs-Platz 18 2024 00333
Sun–Thu 12–3, 6–10, Fri 11.30–3pm U
or S Bahn Marienplatz

ADAMELLO (€)

eiscafe-adamello.de

Tucked away in a quiet backstreet in
Haidhausen, this Italian-run café is
renowned for selling arguably the best
ice cream in town. The pistachio is to
die for while the house specialty, Copa
Adamello, conceals a delicious liqueur.

L8 Preysingstrasse 29 48 32 83
Daily 11–6 (12am in summer) Tram 18

AUGUSTINER GASTSTÄTTEN (€€)

augustiner-restaurant.com

Munich's oldest surviving brewery
premises is now a restaurant and beer
hall serving reasonably priced Bavarian
fare. Beer was still brewed here until
1897. In the summer you can choose
between the Art Nouveau dining room
and the pleasant courtyard terrace.

H7 Neuhauserstrasse 27 2318 3257
U- or S-Bahn Karlsplatz

CAFÉ FRISCHHUT (€)

Early birds meet night owls for strong
coffee and delicious deep-fried
Schmalznudeln donuts as early as five
in the morning. This is a great spot for
relaxing and people-watching.

J7 Prälat-Zistl-Strasse 8 2602 3156
Mon–Fri 7–6, Sat 5–5 U- or S-Bahn
Marienplatz

EINSTEIN (€€€)

einstein-restaurant.de

The culinary flagship of the Jewish
Cultural Center offers sophisticated

KUNSTLERHAUS (€€€)

the-grill-munich.de

Dine out at the stately premises of
Munich's House of Artists, which dates
originally from 1893 and was restored
after World War II. The Grill serves fish
as well as meat dishes and lines sometimes start to build early in the evening
so reservations are advised.

H7 Lenbachplatz 8 4520 5950
Mon–Sat 6pm–12am U- or S-Bahn
Karlsplatz

MÜNCHNER SUPPENKÜCHE (€)

muenchner-suppenkueche.com

Sightseeing on a cold day? Then warm
up with a nourishing bowl of hot soup
at this little eatery. Try the interesting
Pfannkuchen-suppe (pancake soup) or
Leberknödelsuppe (liver dumpling
soup). Vegetarian options are available.

J7 Viktualienmarkt 5527 3390
Shop hours U- or S-Bahn Marienplatz

RUSTIC ATMOSPHERE

For an all-round Bavarian culinary
experience visit the Augustiner Gaststätten,
Nürnberger Bratwurst Glöckl or Schneider
Brauhaus (▷ 41–42). Hearty portions
of *Weisswürste* (white sausages) or
Schweinebraten (roast pork) with sauerkraut and *Knödeln* (dumplings) are served
in warm, faux-rustic surroundings. Expect
to be greeted by picture-framed mountain
scenes, trophy stag antlers, wooden furniture, check tablecloths and beer steins.

NÜRNBERGER BRATWURST GLÖCKL (€)

bratwurst-gloeckl.de

Best known for the *Nürnberger Bratwurst* grilled over an open beech-wood fire and served with sauerkraut, this traditional restaurant has seating in two wood-paneled rooms and also a beer garden on the terrace. Reserve a table if you prefer the more intimate Dürerstube on the first floor.

🚊 J7 ✉ Frauenplatz 9 ☎ 2919 450 🕔 Daily 10am–midnight 🚇 U- or S-Bahn Marienplatz

PRINZ MYSHKIN (€€)

prinzmyshkin.com

Creative vegan and vegetarian dishes are the order of the day in this fashionable café with its striking white interior. Don't miss the tofu stroganoff or the *involtini*, chard roulades filled with nuts and tofu.

🚊 J7 ✉ Hackenstrasse 2 ☎ 26 55 96 🕔 Daily 9.30–1am 🚇 U- or S-Bahn Marienplatz

RATSKELLER (€€)

ratskeller.com

You'll find this classic beer keller with its hallmark vaulted ceiling in the historic New Town Hall (▷ 28–29). Traditional Bavarian fare is to be expected here, along with Löwenbräu beer.

🚊 J7 ✉ Marienplatz 8 ☎ 2199 890 🕔 Daily 9.30–1am 🚇 U- or S-Bahn Marienplatz

SCHLEMMERMEYER (€)

Take a break from sightseeing to lunch at this gourmet delicatessen. Try the hearty Alpine-style open sandwiches or *Leberkäs*.

🚊 J7 ✉ Viktualienmarkt ☎ 295575 🕔 Shop hours 🚇 U- or S-Bahn Marienplatz

SCHNEIDER BRÄUHAUS (€)

schneider-brauhaus.de

The *Weisswürste* here are easily the best in town, or if you are really hungry, rise to the challenge of *Spanferkel* (suckling pig with trimmings). Both go down well with the wickedly strong *Weissbier*.

🚊 J7 ✉ Tal 7 ☎ 2901 380 🕔 Daily 8am–1am 🚇 U- or S-Bahn Marienplatz

VINAIOLO (€€€)

vinaiolo.de

Delightfully decorated and furnished in the style of an early 20th-century Italian grocery store, the food in Vinaiolo is of a uniformly high standard and there is an impressive choice of wines.

🚊 L8 ✉ Steinstrasse 42 ☎ 4895 0356 🕔 Sun–Fri noon–3, 6.30–1, Sat 6.30–1 🚇 S-Bahn Rosenheimer Platz 🚋 Tram 15, 25

ZUM ALTEN MARKT (€€–€€€)

zumaltenmarkt.de

Be transported to the Alpine setting of the South Tyrol in this restaurant specializing in regional cooking. River fish is on offer if you're averse to meat.

🚊 J7 ✉ Dreifaltigkeitsplatz 3 (at Viktualienmarkt) ☎ 29 99 95 🕔 Mon–Sat 11am–midnight

---

MAHLZEIT!

Meals are taken comparatively early in Munich, because most people start work at around 7–8am. Lunch is eaten between 11.15 and 2 and is for many the main meal of the day, followed by a light supper or *Abendbrot* ("evening bread"). Restaurants usually serve dinner between 6pm and 11pm. In the evening it is polite to wish fellow diners *"Guten Appetit."* However, during the day it is more common to hear the word *"Mahlzeit."*

Innenstadt Nord

Soak up the city's unique charm and atmosphere from the royal Residenz to the cobbled streets of the Altstadt surrounding the Hofbräuhaus, and browse in the city's most exclusive shops.

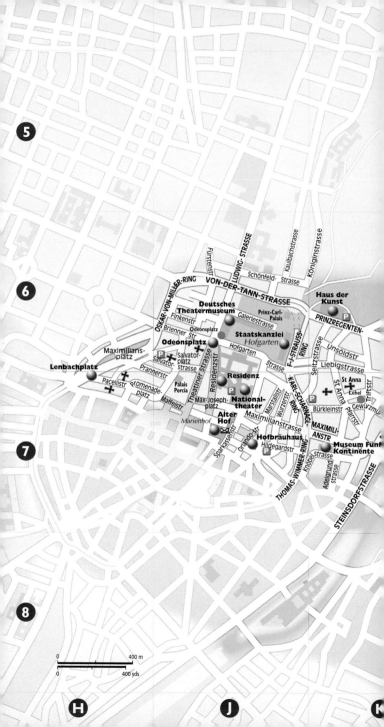

5

6

KAULBACHSTRASSE

KÖNIGINSTRASSE

FÜRSTENSTR

LUDWIG-STRASSE

Schönfeld-

Strasse

VON-DER-TANN-STRASSE

OSKAR-VON-MILLER-RING

Haus der Kunst

PRINZREGENTEN-

Deutsches Theatermuseum

Galeriestrasse

Prinz-Carl-Palais

FINKENSTR

Brienner Str

Odeonsplatz

Staatskanzlei

Hofgarten

F-J-STRAUSS-RING

Unsöldstr

Odeonsplatz

Hofgarten

Seitzstrasse

Lieblgstrasse

Maximilians-platz

Salvatorstrasse

Salvator-platz

Theatiner Strasse

Strasse

Lenbachplatz

PRANNERSTR

Residenzstr

St Anna

Residenz

KARL-SCHARNAGL-RING

Lehel

Pacellistr

Palais Porcia

Max-Joseph-platz

National-theater

Marstallstr

St Anna

Bürkleinstr

Pratrstr

Gewürzmühl

Triftstr

PROMENADE-platz

MAFFEISTR

Maximilianstrasse

Wurzerstr

MAXIMILI-ANSTR

Marienhof

Alter Hof

Orlando-str

Hofbrauhaus

Hildegardstr

Museum Fünf Kontinente

THOMAS-WIMMER-RING

Knöbel-strasse

Sparkassenstr

Adelgund-strasse

STEINSDORFSTRASSE

7

8

0 — 400 m
0 — 400 yds

H **J** **K**

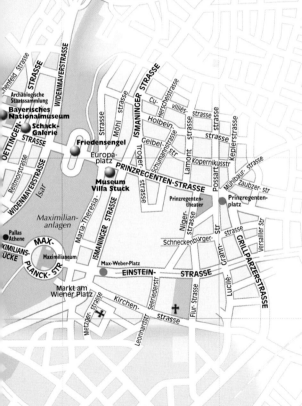

Xhefeld Strasse
STRASSE
WIDENMAYERSTRASSE
Archäologische
Staatssammlung
**Bayerisches
Nationalmuseum**
OETTINGEN-
**Schack-
Galerie**
STRASSE
Reitmorstrasse
WIDENMAYERSTRASSE
Isar
Friedensengel
Europa-
platz
PRINZREGENTEN-STRASSE
**Museum
Villa Stuck**

ISMANINGER STRASSE
Möhl strasse
Cu-
Herschelstrasse
villiés strasse
Holbein.
Geibel-str
Troger
Schumannstrasse
Lamont
strasse
Kopernikusstr
strasse
strasse
Keplerstrasse
Possart
strasse
Mühlbaur- strasse
zaubzer- str
**Prinzregenten-
platz**

Prinzregenten-
theater
Niger-
strasse
Grann- str
strasse
Lucile
versailler str
GRILLPARZERSTRASSE

Maximilian-
anlagen

Maria-Theresia
ISMANINGER STRASSE

Pallas
Athene
AXIMILIANS-
ÜCKE
MAX.-
PLANCK- STR
Maximilianeum
Max-Weber-Platz
EINSTEIN-   **STRASSE**
Schneckenburger-

**Markt am
Wiener Platz**
Metzger- strasse
Kirchen-
strasse
Seerieder str
Leonhardstr
Flur strasse
strasse

L

Bayerisches Nationalmuseum

The Bavarian National Museum was founded by Maximilian II in the 19th century

THE BASICS

bayerisches-national museum.de

🔲 K6

✉ Prinzregentenstrasse 3

☎ 211 2401

🕐 Tue–Sun 10–5 (Thu until 8pm)

🍴 Café

🚇 U-Bahn Lehel

🚌 100; tram 17

♿ Good

💳 Moderate; Sun inexpensive

HIGHLIGHTS

● 16th-century model of Munich, by master wood-carver Jakob Sandtner
● Augsburg Weaving Room
● Tilman Riemenschneider sculptures
● Crib collection
● Flanders Tapestry Room
● Weaponry Room
● Closet from Palais Tattenbach

The Bavarian National Museum is one of Europe's leading visual museums and is guaranteed to give you a real taste of Bavarian cultural life over the centuries to the present day.

Wittelsbach treasures The Wittelsbach rulers' passion for collecting works of art led to the founding of the museum in 1885 by Maximilian II; it transferred to its present site in 1900. Even the building mirrors the various periods represented within the museum: the west wing is Romanesque, the east wing Renaissance, the tower baroque and the west end rococo. The interior is divided into two main collections—Folklore and Art History—providing a comprehensive survey of German cultural history, both sacred and secular, from the early Middle Ages to the present.

Folklore A series of rooms authentically decorated with rustic Bavarian furniture, glass, pottery and woodcraft provides a wonderful insight into rural life of bygone years. The Augsburg Room, with its outstanding carved ceiling, is particularly attractive. The museum is famous for its sculptures by Hans Leinberger, Ignaz Günther and Tilman Riemenschneider and its large crib collection.

Art history This collection is divided into specialist departments including Bavarian traditional costume, tapestries, porcelain, jewelry, armor and the largest ivory collection in Europe.

Hofbräuhaus is the spiritual home of Bavarian beer

N="1"

No trip to Munich is complete without a visit to the Hofbräuhaus, despite its being a tourist honeypot, to sip a cool beer in the shady courtyard or in the lively beer hall. The Hofbräuhaus was founded by Wilhelm V in 1589.

Royal beer The brewery produced a special dark ale for Wilhelm's court, because he disliked the expensive local beer. Beer in Bavaria had been considered an aristocratic drink ever since the harsh winters of the 14th century destroyed the Bavarian vineyards. The ordinary citizens were unable to taste this royal brew until 1828, when the brewery finally became an inn.

Battle of the Hofbräuhaus The first mass meeting of the National Socialist Workers' Party (later the Nazi Party) was held in the Hofbräuhaus in 1920. It soon became regarded as the city's most prestigious political beer-hall arena. Here Hitler established himself as a powerful orator. On 4 November 1921, his storm troops first gained notoriety in a huge brawl, later known as the *Schlacht im Hofbräuhaus* (Battle of the Hofbräuhaus). Despite the hurling of chairs and mugs, Hitler finished his speech.

Germany's most famous pub Undoubtedly the city's best-known institution after the *Oktoberfest*, and a meeting place for visitors from all over the world, the Hofbräuhaus—with its long tables, dirndl-clad waitresses and jolly Bavarian music—is a must for tourists.

THE BASICS

hofbraeuhaus.de
🔖 J7
✉ Am Platzl 9
☎ 2901 3610
🕐 Daily 9am–12am. Brass band 11am–3pm, 5.30–midnight
🚇 U- or S-Bahn Marienplatz
🚌 52, 131; tram 19
♿ Good

DID YOU KNOW?

● The Munich Beer Regulations of 1487 are the oldest written food laws in the world.
● Bavaria is home to some 600 breweries.
● The Hofbräuhaus has its very own drinking song: *"In München steht ein Hofbräuhaus, eins, zwei, drei, g'suffa"*... (one, two, three and down the hatch).

Nationaltheater

The fully restored Nationaltheater, inside and out

THE BASICS

bayerische.staatsoper.de
J7
Max-Joseph-Platz 2
21 85 01
Box office Mon–Sat
10–7; Marstallplatz 5;
tel: 2185 1920
U- or S-Bahn
Marienplatz, U-Bahn
Odeonsplatz
52, 100; tram 19
Few
Tour 2pm, days vary:
moderate

HIGHLIGHTS

Outside
● Facade
● Pediment with *Apollo and the Muses*, Georg Brenninger, 1972
● Pediment with glass mosaic of *Pegasus with the Horae*, Leo Schwanthaler, 19th century
Inside
● Auditorium
● Royal box
● High-tech stage machinery and backstage equipment
● Prompter's box
● Foyer

Munich's Nationaltheater ranks among the world's leading opera houses. One of the few German theaters to have been restored to its magnificent pre-war grandeur, it is definitely worth the visit, even if opera is not your scene.

People's opera house The Nationaltheater has been home to the world-famous Bayerische Staatsoper (Bavarian State Opera) since 1818. After wartime bombing its distinguished Greek-temple design with a simple colonnaded facade stood in ruins for years until a group of citizens raised funds to restore it to its former glory. It was reopened in 1963.

Behind the scenes Join a fascinating hour-long tour to take a rare glimpse backstage. The grandiose auditorium, with five tiers of seating decorated in plush red, gold, ivory and dove blue, is crowned by an enormous chandelier, which magically disappears into the ceiling when the curtain rises. The impressive foyer rooms provide an elegant setting for the audience to promenade in their finery.

Opening nights Many important operas have been premiered here over the centuries, including five by Wagner during the reign of Ludwig II. Many eminent artists have conducted, directed and performed here in a repertoire ranging from Munich favorites—Mozart, Wagner and Strauss—to exciting new commissions from contemporary German composers.

Odeonsplatz

Views of Feldherrnhalle (building on left) and Theatinerkirche (right) on Odeonsplatz

Monumental buildings surround this spacious square at the start of the city's two finest boulevards. Rubbing the noses of the lions guarding the entrance to the Residenz is said to bring good luck.

Grand plan for urban expansion Ludwig I entrusted the layout of Odeonsplatz to Leo von Klenze in the early 19th century to demonstrate the wealth of his flourishing kingdom. It also shows Klenze's passion for Renaissance Italy. His neoclassical Leuchtenberg-Palais (today the Bavarian Ministry of Finance) was inspired by Rome's Palazzo Farnese, and set the pattern for the development of the magnificent Ludwigstrasse.

Feldherrnhalle Apart from the striking Theatinerkirche—Bavaria's first baroque building and for many the most beautiful church in Munich—perhaps the most imposing building in Odeonsplatz is the Feldherrnhalle (Military Commander's Hall). It was commissioned by Ludwig I, and designed by Friedrich von Gärtner as a tribute to the Bavarian army, and adorned with statues of Bavarian generals. Note the faces of the two bronze lions: one is said to be growling at the Residenz (▷ 50–51) while the other, facing the church, remains silent.

The Court Garden The peaceful Hofgarten— a park beside Odeonsplatz—retains its original 17th-century Italian layout of beautifully tended flower beds and fountains.

THE BASICS

➕ J6
🍴 Hofgarten Café
🚇 U-Bahn Odeonsplatz
🚌 100

HIGHLIGHTS

- Theatinerkirche
- Feldherrnhalle
- Hofgarten
- Leuchtenberg-Palais
- Odeon
- Ludwig I monument
- Preysing Palais
- Staatskanzlei (▷ 53)

INNENSTADT NORD TOP 25

Residenz

- Cuvilliés-Theater
- Antiquarium
- Ahnengalerie
- Hofkapelle
- Pavilion Hofgarten
- Bronze Mannerist sculptures

TIP

● Try to attend one of the summer open-air concerts at the Residenz, held in the Brunnenhof courtyard. Contact München Ticket Hotline (tel: 93 60 93).

The glittering staterooms of this stunning palace demonstrate the power and wealth of the Wittelsbach dynasty—five centuries of dukes, prince-electors and kings.

Historical evolution Despite devastating damage in World War II, the Residenz was painstakingly reconstructed over four decades to its original state: a harmonious fusion of Renaissance, baroque, rococo and neoclassical styles. As you explore the rooms (around 80 currently open to the public) crammed with treasures, you can trace the centuries of architectural development, as well as the history and lifestyles of the great Wittelsbach family dynasty.

Palace highlights It would take a full day to see everything; if time is limited just see the

Munich's former ducal palace and gardens, the Residenz and Hofgarten, were begun by the Wittelsbachs in 1385 and contain the Antiquarium, the oldest German museum of Greek antiquities

Ahnengalerie (Ancestral Portrait Gallery), hung with paintings of 121 members of the Wittelsbach family; the Hofkapelle and the Reiche Kapelle, two intimate chapels (one for the courtiers and the other for the royal family); the Brunnenhof courtyard with its magnificent fountain; the shell-encrusted Grottenhof courtyard; and the Antiquarium, the largest Renaissance vaulted hall in northern Europe.

Jewel in the crown The restored Cuvilliés-Theater (▷ 57), jewel of the Residenz and the world's finest rococo theater, is a dazzling sight. Built in 1750, it hosted the première of Mozart's *Idomeneo* in 1781. Also, visit the Schatz-kammer (Treasury) to see the crown jewels and one of the finest collections of ecclesiastical and secular treasures in Europe.

THE BASICS

residenz-muenchen.de

➕ J7

✉ Residenzstrasse/
Max-Joseph-Platz 3

☎ 29 06 71

🕐 Daily 10–5 (9–6 in summer)

🚇 U- or S-Bahn Marienplatz, U-Bahn Odeonsplatz

🚌 100; tram 19

♿ Good

👆 Moderate

❓ Porcelain Collection, Royal Apartments of Ludwig I and Nielung Rooms closed for restoration

More to See

ALTER HOF
alter-hof-muenchen.de

With its picturesque tower, oriel window and cobbled courtyard, the Alter Hof was the royal residence (and home to the German Emperor, Louis IV, from 1328) from the late 12th century until the Residenz was built in the late 14th century. Today, part of the largely restored complex contains a restaurant.

➕ J7 ✉ Burgstrasse 8 🕐 Mon–Sat 10–6 🍴 Restaurant (tel: 2424 3733) 🚇 U-Bahn Marienplatz

DEUTSCHES THEATERMUSEUM
deutschestheatermuseum.de

This small but fascinating display of set designs, costumes, props and photographs brings Germany's rich theatrical past to life. The changing temporary exhibitions are usually very interesting and well worth seeing.

➕ J6 ✉ Galeriestrasse 4a ☎ 2106 9128 🕐 Tue–Sun 10–4 🚇 U-Bahn Odeonsplatz 🎫 Moderate

FRIEDENSENGEL
The golden Angel of Peace, high above the River Isar, was built for the 25th anniversary of Germany's victory over France in 1871. There are views from the platform across the Maximilian Park.

➕ L6 ✉ Prinzregentenstrasse 🚌 100; tram 18

HAUS DER KUNST
hausderkunst.de

This once notorious Nazi building—one of the few buildings that Allied bombardments missed—was nick-named the *Weisswurst* (white sausage) gallery by Hitler's opponents, because of its crude neoclassical columns. The pseudo-Classical building, designed by Paul Ludwig Troost, was the first monumental Nazi building in Munich, and set the pattern for later designs. The cellar bar is still decorated in 1930s style. Today, the building provides a forum for modern art exhibitions.

➕ K6 ✉ Prinzregentenstrasse 1

Artwork in the Haus der Kunst

The golden figure of the Friedensengel (Angel of Peace)

☎ 2112 7113 🕙 Daily 10–8 (Thu until 10) 🚇 U-Bahn Lehel 🚌 100; tram 17 🎫 Varies: moderate to expensive

LENBACHPLATZ

In this busy square is Munich's loveliest neoclassical fountain, Wittelsbacher Brunnen (1895). Its two figures symbolize the destructive and healing power of water. Another remarkable gem (no. 8) is the Kunstlerhaus (1911), now a café-restaurant.
✚ H6 ✉ Lenbachplatz 🚇 U-Bahn Karlsplatz

MUSEUM FÜNF KONTINENTE

voelkerkundemuseum-muenchen.de
Germany's oldest ethnography museum holds 150,000 exhibits, from five continents, displayed by region–South America, Africa, India, Oceania and the Islamic Orient. Exhibitions are both thoughtful and thought-provoking.
✚ K7 ✉ Maximilianstrasse 42 ☎ 210 1361 00 🕙 Tue–Sun 9.30–5.30 🍴 Café 🚇 U-Bahn Lehel 🎫 Moderate

MUSEUM VILLA STUCK

villastuck.de
This stunning Jugendstil villa, the former home of artist Franz von Stuck, has been beautifully restored and contains changing exhibitions dedicated to 20th-century art.
✚ L7 ✉ Prinzregentenstrasse 60 ☎ 4555 5105 🕙 Tue–Sun 11–6 🚇 U-Bahn Prinzregentenplatz 🚌 100; tram 18 🎫 Inexpensive

SCHACK-GALERIE

pinakothek.de
This intimate gallery captures the spirit of 19th-century German art.
✚ K6 ✉ Prinzregentenstrasse 9 ☎ 238 0520 🕙 Wed–Sun 10–6 🚇 U-Bahn Lehel 🚌 100; tram 18 🎫 Inexpensive

STAATSKANZLEI

The gleaming glass-and-steel Bavarian State Chancellery building is framed by a Renaissance-style arcade. The dome of the former Army Museum is its focal point.
✚ J6 ✉ Hofgarten 🚇 U-Bahn Odeonsplatz

The Renaissance-style arcade of the Staatskanzlei

Royal Munich

Wind the clocks back and stroll through Royal Munich with its maze of attractive cobbled streets and royal residences.

DISTANCE: 1.3km (0.8 miles) **ALLOW:** 1 hour (excluding visits)

START

ODEONSPLATZ (▷ 49)
🟥 J6 🔲 U-Bahn Odeonsplatz

END

ENGLISCHER GARTEN (▷ 64–65)
🟥 K4 🔲 U-Bahn Universität

1 From Odeonsplatz walk down Theatinerstrasse. Turn left at Marienhof then first right into Dienerstrasse past Alois Dallmayr—the former royal delicatessen (▷ 55)—to Marienplatz (▷ 28–29).

2 From the Old Town Hall, go down Burgstrasse (beside Ludwig Beck department store), the oldest street in the city, past homes of former residents Mozart and Cuvilliés.

3 Go through the archway of the old royal residence (Alter Hof, ▷ 52) and turn right past the Central Mint (Münzhof) along Pfisterstrasse to soak up some true Bavarian atmosphere at the Hofbräuhaus (▷ 47).

4 On leaving the main entrance of the Hofbräuhaus, turn right through Platzl and past Am Kosttor up to the bright lights and dazzling designer windows of exclusive Maximilianstrasse.

8 The famous Englischer Garten (English Garden) (▷ 64–65) is just a stone's throw from the gallery. Head toward the Love Temple, one of the park's great landmarks, for splendid views of Munich's skyline.

7 Cut diagonally across the gardens, past the Staatskanzlei (▷ 53), finished in 1994, and continue down a narrow path alongside the Dichtergarten (Poets' Garden). Cross Von-der-Tann-Strasse by the pedestrian subway to the Haus der Kunst (▷ 52).

6 Head up Residenzstrasse, past the Residenz (▷ 50–51) on your right. Returning to Odeonsplatz, head eastward into the enchanting Hofgarten (Court Garden), with its fountains and formal flower beds.

5 Turn left at Maximilianstrasse toward the magnificently illuminated Nationaltheater (▷ 48) at Max-Joseph-Platz.

Shopping

ANTIKE UHREN EDER

uhreneder.de

This specialist watchmakers of the fifth generation has valuable German timepieces dating from the 19th and 20th centuries. Collectors make a beeline for the pocket watches.

H6 ☒ Lenbachplatz 7 ☎ 22 03 05
U- or S-Bahn Karlsplatz

BOGNER HAUS

This classic Munich company sells every conceivable item of sports clothing for both men and women. Skiers wanting heads to turn on the piste take note as the current owner Willy Bogner Jr supplied the ski costumes for the James Bond movie *For Your Eyes Only*.

J7 ☒ Residenzstrasse 14–15 ☎ 290 7040
U- or S-Bahn Marienplatz

BREE

bree.com

The Bree label has been a byword for quality design for more than 40 years. Shop here for smart suitcases, handbags, backpacks, briefcases and more.

J6 ☒ Theatinerhof, Salvatorstrasse 2
☎ 29 87 45 U-Bahn Odeonsplatz

DALLMAYR

dallmayr.de

Alois Dallmayr is the city's top delicatessen and has been around since 1700 when it served the Bavarian court. You will also find a bar, restaurant and grill on the premises (open during shop hours).

J7 ☒ Dienerstrasse 14–15 ☎ 213 5100
U- or S-Bahn Marienplatz

ED. MEIER

Originally Munich's oldest shoe shop with a history going back to 1596. The spacious revamped store now retails

beautifully tailored smart-casual wear using only the finest materials. Break off from browsing to relax in one of the leather-upholstered armchairs.

J7 ☒ Briennerstrasse 10 ☎ 22 50 02
U-or S-Bahn Marienplatz

ELLY SEIDL

ellyseidl.de

A traditional family business, this tiny chocolate shop is famous for its pralines and *Münchner Kuppeln* chocolates, which are made to resemble the onion-domes of the Frauenkirche. Chocoholics should look no further.

J7 ☒ Maffeistrasse 1 ☎ 22 44 34
U- or S-Bahn Marienplatz

FANSHOP

fcbayern.de

If you haven't got time to get to the Allianz Arena (▷ 101), this city store has everything imaginable to please FC Bayern supporters, from scarves and teddies to clothing and sports bags.

J7 ☒ Orlandostrasse 1 ☎ 69 93 1666
U- or S-Bahn Marienplatz

FEINKOST KÄFER

feinkost-kaefer.de

Paul and Elsa Käfer opened this modest food and wine shop in Munich in 1930. The shop remains a food-lover's paradise—an epicurean labyrinth selling delicious and high-quality food and drink from around the world.

L7 ☒ Prinzregentenstrasse 73 ☎ 416
8247 U-Bahn Prinzregentenplatz

HEMMERLE

hemmerle.de

A long-established family jeweler with a connection to Bavarian royalty. Shop here for expensive, but beautifully crafted, high-quality jewelry—rings,

earrings, bracelets, brooches, necklaces and men's cuff links.

🕂 J7 ✉ Maximilianstrasse 14 ☎ 242 2600
🚋 Tram 19

KUNSTGEWERBEVEREIN

bayerischer-kunstgewerbeverein.de

The Arts and Crafts Association was founded in 1851 to ensure the highest standards for local handicrafts. Shop here for charming carved and painted puppets, pottery, beautiful jewelry, carnival masks, glassware, toys and textiles—a truly exclusive gift.

🕂 H7 ✉ Pacellistrasse 6–8 ☎ 290 1470
🚉 U- or S-Bahn Karlsplatz

LODEN FREY

loden-frey.de

Choose your traditional *Trachten* (Bavarian folk costume, see panel) from an extensive selection here of blouses, skirts, dresses, shorts and jackets; also shoes, hats and other accessories. New designs appear each season.

🕂 J7 ✉ Maffeistrasse 7–9 ☎ 21 03 90
🚉 U- or S-Bahn Marienplatz

MARKT AM WIENER PLATZ

markt-am-wiener-platz.de

This tiny market has been a permanent feature on the square since 1891. Small green wooden stands cluster local produce around the blue-and-white maypole. Margot's coffee shop and boulangerie is a favorite with locals, while on weekends there are family activities.

🕂 L7 ✉ Wiener Platz 🚉 U-Bahn Max-Weber-Platz

PORZELLAN MANUFAKTUR NYMPHENBURG

nymphenburg.com

If you do not have time to visit the pottery at the Nymphenburg Palace (▷ 84–85), this outlet sells an identical range of traditional rococo porcelain and contemporary handmade designs. The range includes dinnerware, vases, figurines and much more.

🕂 J6 ✉ Odeonsplatz 1 ☎ 28 24 28
🕐 Mon–Fri 10–5 🚉 U-Bahn Odeonsplatz

ROSENTHAL

rosenthal.de

Take your choice from the impressive range of smart, contemporary Rosenthal porcelain and glass, together with other choice designer ware. Styles range from the classic to the striking and modern. This shop is a real delight for those who love stylish tableware.

🕂 J6 ✉ Kardinal-Faulhaber-Straße 5 ☎ 22 26 17 🚉 U-Bahn Odeonsplatz

SCHREIBMAYR

schreibmayr-schreibkultur.de

In 1826, the original Schreibmayr acquired the concession for a book-binding and stationery business from King Ludwig I. This charming outlet still sells "King Ludwig's ink" as well as an elegant range of desktop equipment, pens and handmade paper. With shops like this it's good to know that the art of letter writing is not yet dead.

🕂 J7 ✉ Theatinerstrasse 11 (in the Fünf Höfen) ☎ 219 9840 🚉 U- or S-Bahn Marienplatz

FOLK COSTUME

The nice thing about *Trachten* (Bavarian folk costume) is that Münchners really do wear it, especially on Sundays, holidays or festive occasions. Most popular are the lederhosen and the smart green-collared grey jackets for men or the brightly colored dirndl dresses with fitted bodices and full gathered skirts for women.

Entertainment and Nightlife

JAZZCLUB UNTERFAHRT

unterfahrt.de

One of Europe's most eminent jazz clubs, Unterfahrt features programs by German and international bands in a variety of genres, from traditional to avant-garde; also jam sessions. To plan your evening, consult the website.

➕ L7 ✉ Einsteinstrasse 42 ☎ 448 2794 🕐 Sun–Thu 7.30pm–1am, Fri–Sat 7.30pm–3am 🚇 U-Bahn Max-Weber-Platz 🚊 Tram 19

KOMÖDIE IM BAYERISCHEN HOF

komoedie-muenchen.de

Sophisticated light comedy is the specialty here, while the fun atmosphere promises a good evening out.

➕ H7 ✉ Promenadeplatz 6 ☎ 2916 1633 🚇 U- or S-Bahn Karlsplatz

NATIONALTHEATER

staatstheater.bayern.de

bayerische.staatsoper.de

One of Europe's most important cultural venues (▷ 48) is the home of the State Ballet, Opera and Orchestra, as well as the National Theater. The opera festival in July is a cultural high point.

➕ J7 ✉ Max-Joseph-Platz ☎ 2185 1920 🚇 U- or S-Bahn Marienplatz

P1

p1-club.de

This well-known nightspot attracts the city's most fashionable set (all eager to catch a glimpse of a celebrity or two). International DJs regularly perform sets to a packed out dancefloor.

➕ K6 ✉ Prinzregentenstrasse 1 ☎ 211 1140 🕐 Daily 11pm–4am 🚇 U-Bahn Lehel

PRINZREGENTENTHEATER

prinzregententheater.de

This hulk of a building, which can be seen from the banks of the River Isar, was built in 1900 and was intended to emulate the famous Wagner Festspielhaus in Bayreuth. Today it stages a varied program of plays, concerts and opera perfomances.

➕ L7 ✉ Prinzregentenplatz 12 ☎ 2185 2899 🚇 U-Bahn Prinzregentenplatz

RESIDENZ

residenz-muenchen.de

Here you will find two of Munich's foremost cultural venues. The Cuvilliés-Theater is considered by many to be the finest rococo theater in the world, while the neoclassical Herkulessaal is the city's most impressive concert hall. Check the website for details of forthcoming events.

➕ J7 ✉ Residenzstrasse 1 ☎ 29 06 71 🚇 U-Bahn Odeonsplatz

SCHUMANN'S

schumanns.de

You can choose one of several bars here, depending on your mood and what you are after, whether it's for a cappuccino, a glass of wine or a custom-made cocktail (in consultation with the barman) before your meal in the restaurant where reservations are essential.

➕ J6 ✉ Odeonsplatz 6–7 ☎ 22 90 60 🕐 Mon–Fri 5pm–3am, Sun 6pm–3am 🚊 Tram 19

MUSICAL MECCA

Munich and music go hand-in-hand. The city's connection with Mozart, Wagner and Richard Strauss, not to mention its three symphony orchestras, has made it famous throughout the world. Today, it plays host to major events in the musical calendar including the glamorous Opera Festival and the Summer Concert Season at Nymphenburg Palace.

Where to Eat

BOGENHAUSER HOF (€€€)

bogenhauser-hof.de

Located in a rustic listed building, Bogenhauser is renowned for its French-inspired cuisine and won Bavaria's coveted Gourmet Restaurant of the Year award in 2016. Reservations are a must.
🔲 L7 ✉ Ismaninger Strasse 85 ☎ 98 55 86 🕓 Mon–Fri 12–4pm, 6pm–1am 🚋 Tram 18

CAFÉ LUITPOLD (€€)

cafe-luitpold.de

A traditional Viennese-style café exuding elegance, Luitpold was once frequented by literary types, including Frank Wedekind, author of *Lulu*. Enjoy your coffee in the neo-classical interior, the glass-covered terrace or street side.
🔲 J6 ✉ Brienner Strasse 11 ☎ 242 8750 🕓 Tue–Sat 8am–11pm, Sun–Mon 8–7 🚇 U-Bahn Odeonsplatz

HALALI (€€€)

restaurant-halali.de

Decorated in the style of a traditional country inn with wooden paneling and antler's heads, Halali offers sophisticated regional cooking with a modern flair.
🔲 J6 ✉ Schönfeldstrasse 22 ☎ 28 59 09 🕓 Mon–Fri 12–3, 6–12, Sat 6–12 🚇 U-Bahn Odeonsplatz

HAXNBAUER IM SCHOLASTIKA-HAUS (€€)

kuffler-gastronomie.de

The Scholastikahaus was first mentioned in the 14th century and has been sensitively restored. Watch the cooks turning huge shanks of pork *(Schwein-shax'n)* and suckling pig *(Spanferkel)* over beechwood fires. Portions are huge and will hearten all meat lovers.
🔲 J7 ✉ Sparkassenstrasse 6 ☎ 216 6540 🕓 Daily 11am–12am 🚇 U- or S-Bahn Marienplatz

WELSER KUCHE (€€)

welser-kuche.de

Head to chez-Welser for an evening of convivial fun. You will be attended by serving women in Renaissance costume and entertained by pipers while you dine on wholesome meat and game dishes based on recipes from the 15th and 16th centuries. There is at least one vegetarian dish.
🔲 J6 ✉ Residenzstrasse 27 🕓 29 65 65 🕓 Daily 7pm–12am 🚇 U-Bahn Odeonsplatz

ZUM FRANZISKANER (€€)

zum-franziskaner.de

A traditional Bavarian hostelry, decorated in rustic style and serving reasonably priced home cooking. Vegetarian and fish dishes are available as well as the stand-by sausages and knuckle of pork. You'll need to book ahead during *Oktoberfest*.
🔲 J7 ✉ Residenzstrasse 9 🕓 2318 120 🕓 9.30am–12am, Sun 10am–12am 🚇 U-Bahn Odeonsplatz

---

LEBKUCHEN TRADITION

The 600-year-old tradition of baking *Lebkuchen* is thought to derive from recipes concocted by medieval monks. The biscuits (cookies) are flavored primarily with almonds, honey and spices. The pre-Christmas season is the busiest time for *Lebkuchen* producer Schmidt, when up to three million biscuits are made every day.

Art treasures abound in the tranquil Max suburb, with its many museums and galleries. Trendy Schwabing, beside the Englischer Garten and the university, buzzes with boutiques, bars and restaurants.

Maxvorstadt and Schwabing

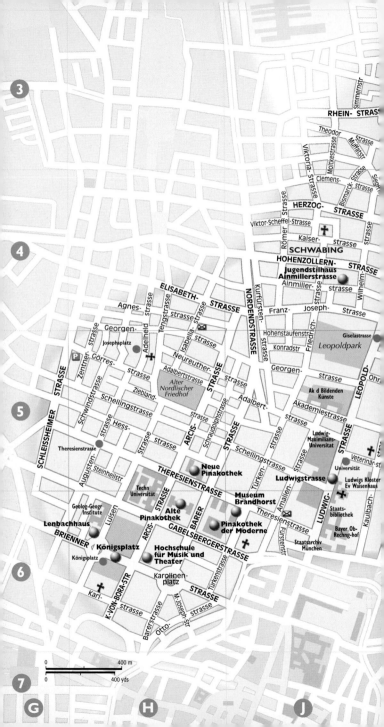

Joh- Fichte- str

Danziger Str

Virchow-

POTSDAMER STR

UNGERERSTRASSE

Driesch str

Gundelindenstr

str

ISAR- RING

STRASSE

Germaniastrasse

Dietlindenstrasse

DIETLINDENSTRASSE

Klementinen-

Wilh-
Ostwaldstrasse

Kunigunden-

strasse

Osterwaldstrasse

Marschallstr

Gohrenstr

strasse

ISAR

RING

Hirschau

Mark

Haimhauser Strasse

Biedersteiner-

Kefer-

strasse

Münchner
Freiheit

Feilitzschstrasse

Gyssling- strasse

P

Sieges strasse

Werneckstrasse

Kleinhesseloher
See

Neues
Seehaus

Nikolei-Str

Seestrasse

Mandlstrasse

M-Josepha-Str

2R

Thiemestr

Englischer
Garten

strasse

Gedonstr

Gisela-
strasse

P

Rumford-
schlössl

asse

Chinesischer
Turm

Am

Tucherpark

IFFLAND

STRASSE

nglin-

Tierärztl
Kliniken

P

Isar

Monopterus

Schwabinger Bach

Oettingenstrasse

Eisbach

Lerchenfeld

Strasse

OETTINGEN STRASSE

WIDENMAYERSTRASSE

K

L

Alte Pinakothek

With more than 850 Old Master artworks, this massive museum, the Old Picture Gallery, is rated alongside the Louvre, Uffizi, Prado and the Metropolitan as one of the world's most important galleries. The Rubens Collection alone is the finest on earth.

Architectural masterpiece The pinnacle of Bavaria's centuries-old dedication to the arts, the gallery was commissioned by Ludwig I and designed by Leo von Klenze to replace the older Kammergalerie in the Residenz, which had become too small for the Royal Collection. Fashioned on the Renaissance palaces of Venice, it took 10 years to construct and on completion in 1836 was proclaimed a master-piece—the largest gallery building of its time and a model for other museum buildings in Rome and Brussels. During World War II it was so badly damaged that demolition of the site was contemplated. Restored in the 1950s and recently given an extensive face-lift, the magnificent gallery provides a fitting backdrop for one of the world's finest collections of Western paintings.

Priceless treasures All the main schools of European art from the Middle Ages to the beginning of the 19th century are represented, with the emphasis on German, Dutch and Flemish paintings, including works by Dürer, van Dyck, Rembrandt and Brueghel, and more than a hundred pieces by Rubens.

THE BASICS

alte-pinakothek.de
➕ H6
✉ Barer Strasse 27
☎ 2380 5122
🕐 Tue 10–8, Wed–Sun 10–6
🚇 U-Bahn Theresienstrasse
🚋 Tram 27
♿ Very good
🏛 Moderate

HIGHLIGHTS

● *Fool's Paradise*, Pieter Brueghel the Elder
● *Four Apostles*, Dürer
● *Adoration of the Magi*, Tiepolo
● *Madonna Tempi*, Raphael
● *The Great Last Judgment*, Rubens
● *The Resurrection*, Rembrandt

Englischer Garten

HIGHLIGHTS

● Chinese Tower
● Kleinhesseloher See and Seehaus
● Monopteros
● Japanese Tea House (tea ceremonies on the second weekend of every month Apr–Oct at 2, 3, 4 and 5pm. Admission charge.)
● Rumford House

TIP

● Enjoy a piping-hot cup of *glühwein*, served at the Chinese Tower in winter.

The English Garden ranks highly on every Münchner's list of preferred city spots. On a sunny day, there's nothing more enjoyable than a stroll in this vast, idyllic park, full of people from all walks of life.

Munich's green lung People come here to enjoy themselves—families boating, musicians busking, children feeding the ducks, New Age groups gathered by the love temple, professionals taking their lunch break, jolly crowds in the packed beer gardens. For this is Munich's beloved green lung—373ha (920 acres) of parkland stretching over 5km (3 miles) along the River Isar.

English influences The English Garden was created by Count Rumford and Ludwig von

The Englischer Garten was Europe's first people's park and is still hugely popular today and offers plenty of recreational activies from cycling, sledging to even surfing on an artifical stream

Sckell in 1789. Breaking away from the French style of manicured lawns and geometrical flower beds, they transformed the Wittelsbach hunting ground into an informal, countrified Volksgarten (people's park).

Attractions Start at the Kleinhesseloher See, an artificial lake with boats for rent. Or spend time relaxing at the Seehaus restaurant before heading south toward the Monopteros, a circular, Greek-style love temple with a splendid view of the park and the distant spires of old Munich. As well as English and Greek influences, the park also has a distinctive oriental tone with its Japanese Tea House and Chinese Tower. Adjacent is the city's most famous beer garden—popular for its brass band, old-fashioned merry-go-round and jovial atmosphere.

THE BASICS

schloesser.bayern.de

✚ K4

🕐 Dawn–dusk

🍴 Chinesischer Turm beer garden, Seehaus restaurant and beer garden (▷ 78), Japanese Tea House, Aumeister restaurant and beer garden

🚇 U-Bahn Odeonsplatz, Universität, Giselastrasse, Münchner Freiheit

🚌 100, 144, 180, 181, 187, 231, 232; tram 17

❓ Rowing boats for hire at Kleinhesseloher See in summer

Königsplatz

HIGHLIGHTS

Glyptothek
● Barberini Faun
● Mnesarete tomb relief
● Aeginetan marbles
● Boy with a goose

Staatliche Antikensammlung
● Exekias' Dionysus cup
● Golden funerary wreath from Armento

TIP

● There are free guided tours of the museums, on Wednesdays at 6pm for the Staatliche Antikensammlung, and on Thursdays at 6pm for the Glyptothek.

This majestic square flanked by three immense neoclassical temples, may come as a surprise in the heart of Munich.

The square and the Propyläen Along with the buildings of Ludwigstrasse, Königsplatz represents Ludwig I's greatest contribution to Munich. Laid out by Leo von Klenze, according to plans created by Carl von Fischer, the square took 50 years to complete, from 1812 to 1862. The final building, the Propyläen, fashioned after the entrance to the Athenian Acropolis, is the most striking.

Nazi control Between 1933 and 1935, the appearance of Königsplatz was completely transformed. Hitler paved over the grassy, tree-lined square and Königsplatz became

The Glyptothek (Sculpture Museum) and Staatliche Antikensammlung (State Collection of Antiquities) on Königsplatz

the National Socialists' "Akropolis Germaniae"—a setting for Nazi rallies. The paving stones have been replaced by broad expanses of lawn, enabling Königsplatz to thankfully return to its former serenity.

Museums The Glyptothek, or Sculpture Museum, on the north flank of Königsplatz is the oldest museum in Munich and one of the most celebrated neoclassical buildings in Germany. Inside is one of Europe's foremost collections of ancient Greek and Roman sculpture. Look for the crowned bust of Emperor Augustus and the mosaic terrace depicting Aion from Sentinum. To the south, the Corinthian-style Staatliche Antikensammlung (State Collection of Antiquities) has a priceless collection of vases, jewelry, bronzes and sculptures.

THE BASICS

antike-am-koenigsplatz.mwn.de

🚇 H6

✉ Königsplatz

☎ Glyptothek and Antikensammlung 2892 7502

🕐 Glyptothek: Tue–Sun 10–5 (Thu until 8); Staatliche Antikensammlung: Tue–Sun 10–5, Wed until 8

🍴 Glyptothek museum café

🚇 U-Bahn Königsplatz

⚫ Good (Glyptothek); none (Antikensammlung)

💰 Moderate

Lenbachhaus

Lenbachhaus is a Florentine Renaissance-style villa

THE BASICS

lenbachhaus.de

✚ H6

✉ Luisenstrasse 33

☎ 2333 2000

🕐 Tue 10–8, Wed–Sun 10–6

🍴 Café and garden terrace

🚇 U-Bahn Königsplatz

♿ Good

💷 Moderate

❓ Audio guides are free with admission tickets

HIGHLIGHTS

● Kandinsky collection
● *Der Blaue Reiter* collection
● *Show your Wound,* Joseph Beuys
● *Blue Horse,* Franz Marc
● Munich Jugendstil collection

This beautiful city gallery displays predominantly 19th- and 20th-century works of art. The tiny formal garden is also a delight—a blend of modern and classical statuary and fountains.

The Lenbachhaus This charming villa was built in 1887 in Florentine High Renaissance style by Gabriel von Seidl for the "painter prince" Franz von Lenbach, darling of the German aristocracy and the most fashionable Bavarian painter of his day. After his death, it became the property of the city and was converted into the municipal art gallery. A north wing was added in the late 1920s to balance the south wing, where Lenbach's studio was housed. The resulting structure perfectly frames the terrace and ornamental gardens.

The collections The chief objective of the gallery is to document the development of painting in Munich from the late Gothic period up to the present day. Munich Romantics and landscape artists are well represented, as is the Jugendstil period. However, it is the paintings by the Munich-based expressionist group known as *Der Blaue Reiter* (Blue Rider) that gained the Lenbachhaus international fame. They include over 300 works by Wassily Kandinsky, who founded the movement with Franz Marc. Paul Klee, Gabriele Münter and August Macke are well represented, and the collection of contemporary art by Kiefer, Warhol, Lichtenstein, Beuys and others is dazzling.

The New Picture Gallery was designed by Alexander von Branca

Neue Pinakothek

The New Picture Gallery is a shining contrast to the Renaissance-style Old Picture Gallery across the road and carries the art collections on through the 19th and early 20th centuries.

A new gallery As with the Old Picture Gallery (Alte Pinakothek ▷ 62–63), it was Ludwig I who instigated the building of this gallery as a home for contemporary art in 1846. However, following extensive damage in World War II, a competition was held in 1966 to design a new gallery to be located in the heart of Schwabing, Munich's bustling student quarter.

Successful design The winning entry, by Munich architect Alexander von Branca, opened in 1981. The concrete, granite and glass structure, sometimes known as the Palazzo Branca, integrates art deco and postmodernist designs with traditional features in an unusual figure-of-eight formation around two inner courtyards and terraced ponds.

Art treasures The Neue Pinakothek contains over 1,000 paintings, drawings and sculptures spanning a variety of periods from rococo to Jugendstil, focusing on the development of German art alongside English 19th-century landscapes and portraits, and French Impressionism. It is best to follow the rooms chronologically, from early Romantic works, then on through French and German late romanticism to French and German Impressionism.

THE BASICS

neue-pinakothek.de
⊞ H5
✉ Barer Strasse 29
☎ 2380 5195
🕓 Wed 10–8, Thu–Mon 10–6
🍴 Restaurant with terrace
🚇 U-Bahn Theresienstrasse
🚋 Tram 27
♿ Very good
💷 Moderate

HIGHLIGHTS

● *Ostende*, William Turner
● *Breakfast*, Edouard Manet
● *Vase with Sunflowers* and *View of Arles*, Vincent van Gogh
● *Large Reclining Woman*, Henry Moore

Pinakothek der Moderne

With four major museums under one roof, the Pinakothek der Moderne, founded in 2002, is regarded as one of the world's greatest collections of 20th- and 21st-century art.

State Gallery of Modern Art Half of the Pinakothek is occupied by modern art, with an exceptional display of paintings, sculptures, video installations and photographic art, plus incomparable collections of German expressionism and surrealism. Works by Magritte, Picasso, Dalí and Warhol characterize 20th-century movements, while more recent trends are represented by Rist, Falvin and Wall.

The New Collection This is one of the leading international collections of applied modern

Private sponsors helped to save the Pinakothek der Moderne when the state ran out of money during its construction. It is now the largest museum structure in Europe

arts—a veritable treasure trove of more than 50,000 items (arranged chronologically) illustrating the history of design, with exhibits ranging from cars to computers and from robots to running shoes. Highlights include the avant-garde of the 1920s and 1930s, function-alism, Pop-Art design and the 1960s space-age.

Architecture Museum The largest collection of its kind in Germany, comprises drawings, photographs and models of more than 700 international architects, displayed in temporary exhibitions examining current architecture.

State Graphic Art Collection Alongside the Architecture Museum are impressive selections from the State Graphics Collection, which has over four milllion etchings and drawings.

THE BASICS

pinakothek-der-moderne.de

🚩 H6

✉ Barer Strasse 40

☎ 2380 5360

🕐 Tue 10–8, Wed–Sun 10–6

🍴 Café-bistro

Ⓤ U-Bahn Königsplatz or Theresienstrasse

🚌 100; tram 27

♿ Very good

💶 Moderate

❓ Free guided tours

More to See

HOCHSCHULE FÜR MUSIK UND THEATER

musikhochschule-muenchen.de

The music academy was designed for Adolf Hitler by Paul Ludwig Troost. It was here that the Munich Agreement was signed by representatives of Germany, Great Britain, Italy and France in September 1938. Hitler's office was above the entrance on the second floor.

✚ H6 ✉ Arcisstrasse 12 ☎ 28903 Ⓤ U-Bahn Königsplatz ❓ Free student concerts held regularly (see website for details)

JUGENDSTILHAUS AINMILLERSTRASSE

Munich's first Jugendstil (art nouveau) house (1900) has been restored to its original glory including the dazzling facade.

✚ J4 ✉ Ainmillerstrasse 22 Ⓤ U-Bahn Giselastrasse

LUDWIGSTRASSE

This grand avenue, leading into Leopoldstrasse, was laid out for Ludwig I. The twin-towered Ludwigskirche contains Peter Cornelius's *Last Judgment*, the largest fresco in the world after Michelangelo's *Last Judgment*. The main landmark on Leopoldstrasse is the 19th-century Siegestor (a triumphal arch topped with a chariot with the figure of Bavaria). Also here is the wacky *Walking Man* sculpture (1995) by Jonathan Borofsky.

✚ J5 ✉ Ludwigstrasse Ⓤ U-Bahn Odeonsplatz, Universität

MUSEUM BRANDHORST

museum-brandhorst.de

The Brandhorst Collection of modern art includes works by European luminaries such as Picasso, Malevich and Schwitters. Its trump card though is American art. There are 100 Andy Warhols for example, as well as works by Cy Twombly, Bruce Naumann and Richard Tuttle.

✚ J6 ✉ Theresienstrasse 35a ☎ 2380 5284 🕐 Tue–Sun 10–6, Thu till 8 Ⓤ U-Bahn Königsplatz, Theresienstrasse 🚌 100; tram 27

The grand staircase in the Hochschule für Musik und Theater

Jugendstilhaus

Galleries and Gardens

This walk takes you past world-class art galleries via Schwabing's fashionable bars and boutiques to the Englischer Garten.

DISTANCE: 1.8km (1.1 miles) **ALLOW:** 2.5 hours (including at least one stop)

 **START** **END**

KÖNIGSPLATZ (▷ 66–67)
✠ H6 🚇 Königsplatz

ENGLISCHER GARTEN (▷ 64–65)
✠ L4 🚇 Münchner Freiheit

❶ Start at the grand and spacious Königsplatz (▷ 66–67), dubbed the "Athens-on-the-Isar" for its grand classical-style architecture.

❽ While away the hours in the English Garden, then head northwards to the boating lake and neighboring Seehaus beer garden (▷ 78).

❷ Here you will find yourself surrounded by museums: choose from the gallery in Lenbachhaus (▷ 68), the Glyptothek (▷ 67) and the Staatliche Antikensammlung (▷ 67).

❼ The university is marked by two fountains. A right turn here will lead you along Veterinärstrasse and into the city's vast green space, the Englischer Garten (▷ 64–65). The Chinese Tower nearby is the site of Munich's most popular beer garden.

❸ Proceed along Briennerstrasse, and turn left into Barer Strasse at the obelisk in Karolinenplatz. This is the heart of the city's Kunstareal (art district), and the surrounding streets are brimming with small private galleries.

❻ The end of Schellingstrasse is marked by the Ludwigskirche, which contains one of the world's largest frescoes. Turn left here into Ludwigstrasse (▷ 72), a grand avenue laid out by Ludwig I.

❹ Before long you will pass by three of its most important galleries: the Alte Pinakothek (▷ 62–63), Neue Pinakothek (▷ 69), and Pinakothek der Moderne (▷ 70–71).

❺ Continue up Barer Strasse then turn right along Schellingstrasse, just one of the maze of streets behind the university, bursting with student life.

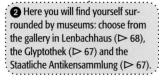
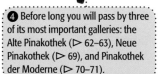

73

Shopping

CHINA'S WORLD

chinasworld.de

This is mainly a specialist outlet for the renowned Rosenthal porcelain. As well as dinner services, however, you will also find silver cutlery, crockery and cheerfully painted coffee mugs.

✚ J5 ✉ Kurfürstenstrasse 15 ☎ 2738 9900
🚇 U-Bahn Universität, Giselastrasse

ELISABETHMARKT

Schwabing's very own produce market has been on this site for more than a hundred years. The old covered market has long gone but among the pavilions here, look for the Milchhäusl (Milk Hut), which dates from the late 19th century and is now a small restaurant with beer garden. The market is also home to one of Munich's best cheese mongers, Le Chalet du Fromage (stand 11).

✚ J4 ✉ Elisabethplatz 🚊 Tram 27

KINDER-AMBIENTE

kinder-ambiente.de

Create the perfect Neverland for your child by visiting this wonderful store which has everything for the young person's bedroom, from babies to teens. On sale are carpets, curtains, desk lamps, toy bags and much else besides.

✚ G5 ✉ Schleissheimer Strasse 73 ☎ 1433 0230 🚇 U-Bahn Josephsplatz

KREMER PIGMENTE

kremer-pigmente.com

A tiny shop opposite the Neue Pinakothek selling, appropriately enough, more than 500 different paint hues for artists in every medium, from oils to watercolors. The aspiring or professional artist will also find paint boxes, brushes, glues and paper.

✚ H6 ✉ Barer Strasse 46 ☎ 28 54 88
🚊 Tram 27

KUNST UND SPIEL

kunstundspiel.de

The educational toys in this colorful store are designed to tap into all a child's senses and to stimulate creativity. They certainly make charming and captivating gifts. Accompanying adults may find something useful in pursuing their own handicraft interests and hobbies, or simply enjoy browsing toys that seem from a simpler age.

✚ K4 ✉ Leopoldstrasse 48 ☎ 381 6270
🚇 U-Bahn Giselastrasse

PERLENMARKT

perlenmarkt.de

This unusual shop sells buttons, beads, pearls and jewelry-making equipment. Browse the trays to collect your own charms for a bracelet, or thread a pair of earrings or a necklace.

✚ J5 ✉ Nordendstrasse 28 ☎ 271 0576
🚊 Tram 27

WORDS' WORTH

wordsworth.de

Forgotten to bring your holiday reading matter with you? Look no further. This store has a wide selection of hardback and paperback titles for adults, as well as a Pooh Corner for children and a section selling British National Trust books.

✚ J5 ✉ Schellingstrasse 3 ☎ 280 9141
🚌 53

TOYS

Germany has been one of the world's leading toy manufacturers since the Middle Ages, and is particularly famous for its china dolls, tin-plate toys and Steiff teddy bears. Many important manufacturing areas are around Munich—Nuremberg, Oberammergau and Berchtesgaden. Today, old Steiff bears are great collector's pieces.

Entertainment and Nightlife

CALL SOUL

call-soul-restaurant-und-bar-schwabing.de

Drop in at this popular bar-kitchen for cocktails, fresh fruit lemonades and international fusion dishes, from soups and salads to tapas and pasta. The menu also includes vegetarian and vegan options. Look out for the cabaret evenings and other live events.

➕ K4 ✉ Biedersteiner Strasse 6 ☎ 4520 6655 ⓘ Mon–Thu 6pm–11pm, Fri–Sat 6pm–2am ⓠ Münchner Freiheit

HOCHSCHULE FÜR MUSIK UND THEATER

musikhochschule-muenchen.de

Young, up-and-coming musicians from the Music Academy (▷ 72) give regular free evening concerts and lunchtime recitals here. You could even drop in on master classes if you wish. Call or check the website for event details.

➕ H6 ✉ Arcisstrasse 12 ☎ 28903 ⓠ U-Bahn Königsplatz

MARIONETTEN-THEATER KLEINES SPIEL

kleinesspiel.de

This delightful theater was founded in 1947 when it was licensed by the American occupying forces as a means to restore traditional cultural values. The puppet shows are conceived with adults in mind and the repertoire includes classics by Bertolt Brecht, Ludwig Thoma, Ben Jonson and others. Shows usually take place on Thursdays at 8pm and are free, but donations are encouraged.

➕ H5 ✉ Neureutherstrasse 12 ☎ 272 3364 ⓠ Tram 27

MÜNCHNER SOMMERTHEATER

muenchner-sommertheater.de

Each July the Munich Summer Theater presents a series of popular open-air performances in the Englischer Garten's amphitheater. Check online for details.

➕ K5 ✉ Rümelinstrasse 8 ☎ 98 93 88 ⓠ U-Bahn Alte Heide ⓠ 187

RENNBAHN

rennbahn-schwabing.com

The group of young friends who have been running this bar for some time now, claim it is one of the last genuine *kneipen* (pubs) in an area of Schwabing that is fast gentrifying. Enjoy the beer and cocktails in a bustling, friendly atmosphere.

➕ K4 ✉ Feilitzstrasse 12 ☎ 394 874 ⓘ Tue–Wed 7pm–2am, Thu 7pm–3am, Fri–Sat 7pm–4am ⓠ U-Bahn Münchner Freiheit

ROTE SONNE

rote-sonne.com

Calling all fans of techno music (also punk, disco and trash) to join fellow aficionados on the crowded dance floor where the music is provided by DJs on some nights, live bands on others. You may have to stand in line to get in.

➕ H6 ✉ Maximiliansplatz 5 ☎ 5526 3330 ⓘ Thu–Sat 11pm–7.30am ⓠ U-Bahn Konigsplatz

BEER GARDENS

The Bavarian capital city's renowned beer gardens thrive from the first warm days of spring to the annual drinking climax of the *Oktoberfest* (▷ 92), when they are augmented by huge party tents erected on a city meadow (Theresienwiese, ▷ 88). Before electrical refrigeration was invented, brewers planted chestnut trees above their storage cellars to help keep supplies cool, then put out tables and benches in the shade to welcome drinkers. To this day, the spring-flowering of the chestnut trees heralds the start of the beer garden season.

Where to Eat

PRICES	
Prices are approximate, based on a 3-course meal for one person.	
€€€	over €50
€€€	€25–€50
€	under €25

BACHMAIER HOFBRÄU (€)

bachmaier-hofbraeu.de

This bar-restaurant offers the usual Bavarian standbys as well as a selection of international dishes; also Sunday brunch (10am–3pm). In the summer most customers head for the terrace.
➕ K4 ✉ Leopoldstrasse 50 ☎ 3838 680
🕐 Mon–Thu 11am–1am, Fri 11am–3am, Sat 10am–3am, Sun 10am–1am 🚇 U-Bahn Giselastrasse

CAFÉ ALTSCHWABING (€)

altschwabing.com

Founded in 1887 and frequented back in the day by artists, writers and politicians, including Wassili Kandinsky, Rainer Maria Rilke and Lenin, the café has preserved its genteel atmosphere.
➕ H5 ✉ Schellingstrasse 56 ☎ 273 1022
🕐 Daily 9am–1am 🚋 53; tram 27

CAFÉ IGNAZ (€)

ignaz-cafe.de

A vegetarian café with a large pleasant terrace and friendly staff, serving some great vegetarian pizzas and risotto. Ignaz also sells delicious cakes and pastries and there is a buffet on weekends.
➕ H5 ✉ Georgenstrasse 67 ☎ 271 6093
🕐 Mon, Wed–Fri 8am–10pm, Tue 11–10, Sat, Sun 9am–10pm 🚇 U-Bahn Josephsplatz

CAFÉ JOON (€)

cafejoon.de

Plenty of healthy brunch options are available at this popular student haunt, from muesli to pureed avocado and poached egg on toast. The freshly pressed lemonade goes down a treat.
➕ H5 ✉ Theresienstrasse 114 ☎ 415 50941
🕐 Wed–Sat 9am–1am, Sun 9–8, Mon–Tue 9am–11pm 🚇 U-Bahn Theresienstrasse

CAFÉ REITSCHULE (€€)

cafe-reitschule.de

Watch the horses practice as you eat in the historic Riding School. There is a special breakfast menu on weekends (9–3pm), otherwise you can eat à la carte from the international menu; either way, enjoy the views of the English Garden from the terrace. Tables are at a premium so ensure you book ahead.
➕ K5 ✉ Königinstrasse 34 ☎ 388 8780
🕐 Daily 9am–1am 🚇 U-Bahn Giselastrasse

LEMAR (€€)

lemar-restaurant.de

The Sadat brothers started Lemar nearly 20 years ago to cater for the growing Afghan community. Guests dine in tasteful, subdued surroundings on predominantly lamb-based dishes, served with fresh vegetables and rice, and infused with heavenly herbs.
➕ J4 ✉ Viktor-Scheffel-Strasse 23 ☎ 39 76 77 🕐 Daily 5pm-12am 🚋 Tram 12, 27; bus 53

SECOND BREAKFAST
As many people in Munich start their working day very early, they often indulge in a mid-morning snack to bridge the gap between breakfast and lunch, called *Brotzeit* (bread time). This may be a sandwich or the traditional local specialty of boiled *Weisswürste* (white sausages) and *Brezen* (pretzels, knotted rolls sprinkled with coarse grains of salt).

MAX EMANUEL BRÄUEREI (€)

max-emanuel-brauerei.de

Founded in the 1880s, these brewery premises have since been revamped, while retaining the reputation for homely Bavarian cooking. A definite plus is the spacious summer terrace and there are music events in the evenings.

➕ J5 ✉ Adalbertstrasse 33 ☎ 271 5158 🕐 Daily 11–11 (evenings only in winter) 🚇 U-Bahn Universität

THE POTTING SHED (€€)

the-potting-shed.de

Anything but tinkering in the kitchen here, as the chef is deadly serious about producing the highest-quality gourmet burgers (including a vegetarian option).

➕ K4 ✉ Occamstrasse 11 ☎ 3407 7284 🕐 Tue–Sat 6pm–2am 🚇 U-Bahn Münchner Freiheit

SCHELLING SALON (€–€€)

schelling-salon.de

For over 140 years this famous Munich café has served Leberkäse, Knödel and other traditional fare to a motley clientele, including Adolf Hitler and the former Bavarian Minister-President, Franz Josef Strauss.

➕ H5 ✉ Schellingstrasse 34 ☎ 2720 788 🕐 Mon, Thu–Sun 10am–1am 🚇 U-Bahn Universität

SEEHAUS IM ENGLISCHEN GARTEN (€€)

kuffler-gastronomie.de

A smart, modern restaurant decorated in the style of a Bavarian Stübl (homely dining room) located in the heart of the English Garden and overlooking the boating lake. Places on the terrace are coveted so book ahead or come early.

➕ L4 ✉ Kleinhesselohe 3 ☎ 38 16 130 🕐 10am–1am 🚇 U-Bahn Münchner Freiheit

SEOUL (€€)

seoulrestaurantmunich.com

Possibly the best of Munich's Korean restaurants, Seoul focuses on traditional dishes like jeon-gol (a spicy hot pot), kimchi (fermented cabbage with radish) and bulgogi (finely sliced marinated beef) served unusually with seafood.

➕ K4 ✉ Leopoldstrasse 122 ☎ 34 81 04 🕐 Lunch, dinner; closed 1st, 3rd Mon of month 🚇 U-Bahn Münchner Freiheit

TANTRIS (€€€)

tantris.de

With two Michelin stars, this is arguably Munich's top restaurant.serving international cuisine with detectable French-Swiss influences.

➕ K3 ✉ Johann-Fichte-Strasse 7 ☎ 361 9590 🕐 Tue–Sat lunch, dinner 🚇 U-Bahn Dietlindenstrasse

TRESZNJEWSKI (€€)

tresznjewski.com

The arty decor in this brasserie reflects its proximity to the Neue Pinakothek (▷ 69). Known simply as "Treszi" to its regulars, it is packed from breakfast into the wee small hours. The three-course set menu is good value and the beer is supplied by the local brewery, Aying.

➕ H5 ✉ Theresienstrasse 72 ☎ 28 23 49 🕐 Daily 8am–3am 🚋 Tram 27

WALDFEE (€€)

waldfeemuenchen.de

Easy to spot with its signature pink decor, the "Wood Fairy", a popular Austrian eatery, serves Viennese and regional staples like veal schnitzel and Tafelspitz (boiled beef served with pureed apples and horseradish).

➕ K4 ✉ Occamstrasse 13 ☎ 8400 8310 🕐 Sun–Thu 11am–12am; Fri–Sat 11am–1am 🚇 Münchner Freiheit

There's plenty to see in Munich's western suburbs, from the high-tech world of BMW and the Olympiapark to Germany's finest baroque palace at Nymphenburg.

Sights	**82–88**	Top 25		**TOP 25**
Walk	**89**			
Shopping	**90**	Olympiapark ▷ **82**		
Entertainment and Nightlife	**91**	Schloss Nymphenburg ▷ **84**		
		BMW Museum ▷ **86**		
Where to Eat	**92**			

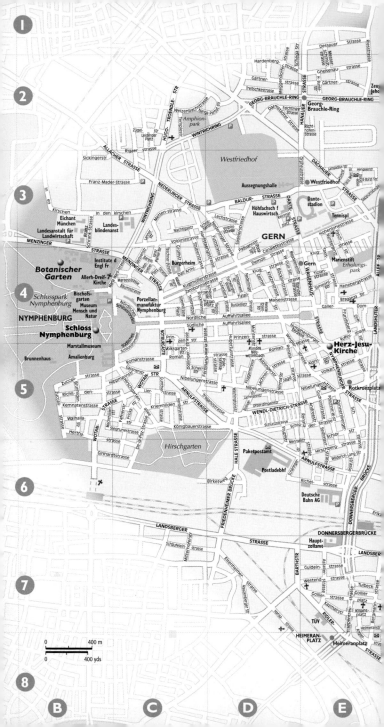

Olympisches Dorf

RIESENFELD

Zentrale Hochschulsportanlage

OLYMPIAPARK

Olympiazentrum

BMW-Hochhaus

Petuelring

Tennisanlage

BMW Museum

PETUELRING

Karmelit-Kloster

GEORG-BRAUCHLE-RING

Olympia-Eisstadion

Olympia halle

Olympiaturm

Olympia-stadion

Olympia Schwimm-halle

Luitpoldpark

Scheidplatz

Radstadion

Olympiapark

Ost-West-Friedenskirche

KARL-

THEODOR-

BELGRAD-

Bayern-platz

Tierklinik

WEST SCHWABING

Arbeitsgericht

HERZOG-

Rosa-Luxemburg-Platz

SCHWERE-

REITER-

STRASSE

Hohenzollernplatz

ELISABETH-

HOHENZOLLERN-

STRASSE

NEUHAUSEN

SCHLEISSHEIMER STRASSE

GABELSBERGERSTRASSE

NYMPHENBURGER

Maillingerstrasse

Stiglmaier-platz

BRIENER STRASSE

MARSSTRASSE

Luisen-Gymn

ARNULFSTRASSE

HACKERBRÜCKE

ELISENSTRASSE

Kinder- und Jugendmuseum

HAUPTBAHNHOF

Hauptbahnhof

BAYER-

STRASSE

SCHWANTHALER STRASSE

Adolf Kolping Str

WESTEND

ESTEND

Theresienwiese

LUDWIGSVOR-STADT

Augenklinik d Universität

Physiolog Institut der Universität

St Elisab

HEIMERANSTRASSE

Schwanthalerhöhe

Anatomie

Pharmakolog

Chirurg Klinik

Bavariapark

Theresienwiese

Psychiatr Klinik

LINDWURMSTRASSE

Klinikum der Innenstadt

Matthias-Pschorr-Strasse

Goetheplatz

Frauenklinik d Universität

F   G   H   J

Olympiapark

DID YOU KNOW?

● The Olympic Park covers more than 3sq km (1sq mile).
● The Olympiaturm is 290m (950ft) high.
● The Olympic Stadium holds 63,000 people.
● The Olympic Village houses about 9,000 people.

TIPS

● The stadium roof climb tour also offers abseiling.
● Children will love the Sea Life aquarium.

Since the 1972 Olympics, the park, with its intriguing skyline, has become one of the city's landmarks. Its tower offers an unforgettable view of Munich and the Alps.

The Games The historic Oberwiesenfeld was a former royal Bavarian parade ground north of the city. In 1909 the world's first Zeppelin airship took off here, and from 1925 until 1939 it was Munich's airport. Abandoned during World War II, it was transformed in 1968 into a multifunctional sport and recreation area. In 1972 it hosted the 20th Summer Olympic Games.

The buildings The television tower here, now called the Olympiaturm, built between 1965 and 1968, is the tallest reinforced concrete

Olympiapark was built for the Summer Olympics in 1972, the viewing platform of the Olympiaturm (Olympic Tower), at 190m (623ft), offers stunning panoramas

construction in Europe. When the weather is clear, the viewing platform and revolving restaurant give a breathtaking panorama of the Alps; the view of the city at night is magical. The stadium's futuristic tent-roof looks like an immense spider's web. When you tour the area on a little train you will see the Olympiasee, a huge artificial lake; the Olympiaberg, a 53m (174ft) hill constructed from wartime rubble; the quaint Russian Orthodox chapel built by Father Timofej, a Russian recluse, beautifully decorated inside with thousands of pieces of silver paper (▷ 88); and the Olympic Village (▷ 87), remembered sadly today as the scene of the terrorist attack on 5 September 1972, in which 11 Israeli athletes and coaches and a German police officer were killed. A memorial to the 12 victims was unveiled in 2017.

THE BASICS

olympiapark-
muenchen.de

✚ G3

✉ Spiridon-Louis-Ring 21

☎ 30670

🕐 Olympiaturm daily 9–midnight. Olympiastadion summer 9–8, winter 9–4

🍴 Revolving restaurant

Ⓤ U-Bahn Olympiazentrum

🚌 173, 177, 178; tram 20, 21

♿ Inexpensive (Stadium without tour). Moderate (Stadium with tour, Tower)

Schloss Nymphenburg

HIGHLIGHTS

- Amalienburg
- Badenburg
- Gallery of Beauties
- Porcelain Museum
- Magdalenenklause
- Marstallmuseum
- Botanical Garden
  (▷ 87)

TIPS

- On weekends, the gardens are especially popular.
- Be sure to visit the Badenburg, said to be Europe's first post-Roman heated pool.

It is hard to believe that one of Germany's largest baroque palaces, set in stunning parkland, began as a modest summer villa.

The palace Five generations of Bavarian royalty were involved in the palace's construction, starting with Elector Ferdinand Maria. Thrilled by the birth of his heir Max Emanuel, he had the central section built for his wife, Henriette Adelaide of Savoy, commissioning an Italian-style villa by Agostino Barelli in 1664. The villa was completed 10 years later. Each succeeding ruler then added to the building, resulting in a majestic, semicircular construction, stretching 500m (550yds) from one wing to the other.

The interior The central structure contains sumptuous galleries, including Ludwig I's Gallery

of Beauties, featuring 36 Munich ladies, some said to have been the king's mistresses. In the old stables, the Marstallmuseum's dazzling collection of state carriages and sleighs recalls the heyday of the Wittelsbach family. The Porcelain Museum provides a comprehensive history of the famous Nymphenburg porcelain factory (▷ 90) since its foundation in 1747.

Park and pavilions Originally in Italian then French baroque style, the gardens were transformed in 1804–23 into a fashionable English park with ornate waterways, statues, pavilions and a maze. See yourself reflected ten-fold in the Hall of Mirrors in the Amalienburg hunting lodge and visit the impressive shell-encrusted interior of the Magdalenenklause hermitage.

THE BASICS

schloss-nymphenburg.de

🔡 B4

☎ 17 90 80

🕐 Palace: Apr to mid-Oct daily 9–6; mid-Oct to Mar 10–4. Park: Jan–Mar, Nov, Dec daily 6–6; Apr, Oct 6–8; May–Sep 6–9.30

🍴 Café Palmenhaus

🚇 U-Bahn Rotkreuzplatz

🚌 51; tram 12, 16, 17

♿ None

👆 Moderate

BMW Museum

The BMW Museum

THE BASICS

bmw-museum.de

🔟 G2

✉ Am Olympiapark 2
(Petuelring)

☎ 1250 16001

🕐 Tue–Sun 10–6

🚇 U-Bahn
Olympiazentrum

🚌 36, 41, 43, 81, 136,
184

♿ Excellent

💰 Expensive

❓ Guided tours in
German and English (60
minutes) 10.15–4.30

HIGHLIGHTS

- 1899 Wartburg Motor Wagon
- 1923 R32 motorcycle
- 1931 Cabriolet
- 1934 Roadster
- 1936 BMW 328
- 1952 The Baroque Angel (BMW 501)
- 1955 BMW 507 roadster
- 2014 H2R Hydrogen car

Showcasing the world-famous BMW brand, this state-of-the-art museum has visitors marveling at the developments in transport technology over the past five generations and into the future.

The museum The BMW Time Horizons Exhibition, housed in a half sphere, provides an eye-catching contrast to the adjacent high-rise headquarters of BMW (▷ 87). Over a quarter of a million visitors come to the BMW Museum annually to see its rare cars and motorcycles. A film, *Das weisse Phantom* (*The White Phantom*), about motorcycle-race world champion Ernst Jakob Henne, brings the world of motorcycle racing to life. As well as vintage BMW models, there are also insights into the past through slides and videos covering such subjects as changing family life and work conditions, the role of women in industry, and car recycling (where BMW is at the forefront of development). There are also unexpected displays such as the BMW Art Cars, where famous artists have designed the paintwork.

Future vision Take a simulated journey into the future with electric or solar-generated hydrogen cars or design your own model and watch it develop on computers. Visitors vie with each other to sit in the cockpit of tomorrow's car and experiment with its data and information systems. Just across Lerchenauer Strasse is the futuristic BMW Welt building, where buyers can collect direct from the factory.

More to See

BMW-HOCHHAUS
This 100m (328ft) tall silver skyscraper resembles a four-leaf clover to some, to others a BMW 4-cylinder engine. It opened in 1973 and was designed by Viennese architect Karl Schwanzer.

⊞ G2 ✉ Petuelring 130 🚇 U-Bahn Petuelring ❓ Phone in advance for a factory tour

BOTANISCHER GARTEN
botmuc.de
The Botanical Garden lies at the northern end of the Nymphenburg Park (▷ 84–85) and its outdoor gardens and greenhouses cover 20ha (50 acres). The gardens are in full bloom from May to June.

⊞ B4 ✉ Menzinger Strasse 65 ☎ 1786 1310 🕐 Nov–Jan daily 9–4.30; Feb–Mar, Oct 9–5; Apr, Sep 9–6; May–Aug 9–7 🍴 Café 🚊 Tram 12 💲 Inexpensive

HERZ-JESU-KIRCHE
herzjesu-muenchen.de
The Heart of Jesus Church was completely rebuilt after a fire destroyed the old church in 1994. The new architectural wonder lays claim to the largest church doors in the world, while the facade is covered in glass panels. On the portal wings the Passion of Christ is depicted in a series of iconographical images.

⊞ E5 ✉ Lachnerstrasse 8 ☎ 130 6750 🕐 Wed–Sun 8–6, Tue 8–12pm 🚇 U-Bahn Rotkreuzplatz 💲 Free ❓ Regular concerts; see website for details.

KINDER- UND JUGENDMUSEUM
kindermuseum-muenchen.de
There is a wide variety of hands-on activities and exhibitions here to delight children and young people. The aim is to promote active learning and awaken curiosity.

⊞ G6 ✉ Arnulfstrasse 3 ☎ 5404 6440 🕐 Tue–Fri 2–5.30, Sat, Sun 11–5.30 🚇 Hauptbahnhof 💲 Moderate

OLYMPISCHES DORF
During the Summer Olympics of 1972, athletes from around the

Botanischer Garten at the north end of the Nymphenburg Park

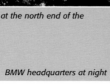

BMW headquarters at night

world stayed in the apartments and bungalows here in the Olympic Village. Most are now private homes.

➕ F1 Ⓤ U-Bahn Olympiazentrum

OST-WEST-FRIEDENSKIRCHE

This unusual Russian Orthodox church was built with rubble from World War II and decorated with tin cans, sweet wrappers and silver chocolate paper, by the Russian hermit Father Timofej, who lived in a hut here for decades. When ordered to leave to make way for the Olympic riding stadium, he protested with the help of some Munich citizens and the stadium was built elsewhere.

➕ F3 Ⓤ U-Bahn Olympiazentrum

SCHLOSS BLUTENBURG

blutenburg.de

A moated 15th-century castle in Obermenzing, the romantic Schloss Blutenburg was originally built as a love-nest for Agnes Bernauer by her secret lover, Duke Albrecht III, in 1438. Sadly, shortly after completion of the magical castle, she was accused of being a witch and was drowned in the Danube at Straubing. This one-time Wittelsbach summer residence has a beautiful chapel, lovely grounds and a renowned collection of more than 500,000 children's books.

➕ Off map to west ✉ Seldweg 15, Obermenzing ☎ 17 90 80 🕐 Chapel daily Apr–Sep 9–5; Oct–Mar 10–4. Library Mon–Fri 2pm–6pm Ⓢ S-Bahn Obermenzing 🎟 Free admission to chapel

THERESIENWIESE

"Theresa's fields" are best known as the venue for the world's biggest beer festival—the *Oktoberfest*. It all began in 1810 with the wedding party of Crown Prince Ludwig and Princess Theresa—a lavish affair with horse racing, shooting matches and a fair but, ironically, no beer. Here too is the 18m (60ft) high Statue of Bavaria; climb the 112 steps inside for great city views.

➕ F8 ✉ Theresienwiese Ⓤ U-Bahn Theresienwiese

Schloss Blutenburg

Oktoberfest *at* Theresienwiese

Green Munich

Escape the bustling city center to visit Schloss Nymphenburg and its gardens, followed by a canal-side stroll to the Olympiapark.

DISTANCE: 3.5km (2.2 miles) **ALLOW:** all day (including visits)

START

END

ROTKREUZPLATZ
🕇 E5 🚇 U-Bahn Rotkreuzplatz

OLYMPIAPARK (▷ 82–83)
🕇 G3 🚇 U-Bahn Olympiapark

❶ Start at Rotkreuzplatz, and head northward up Nymphenburger Strasse. After a short distance, turn left down Lachnerstrasse past the Herz-Jesu-Kirche (▷ 87).

❽ From here, it is a 2.5km (1.5 mile) walk through quiet, green suburbs, following the course of the canal all the way to the Olympiapark (▷ 82–83).

❷ Just past the church, turn right into Winthirstrasse. At the junction with Romanstrasse, note the ornamental Jugendstil (art nouveau) facade at No. 5 (to your right).

❼ Return to the canal via the Nordliche Schlossrondell, past the famous Porzellan Manufaktur Nymphenburg. At Ludwig-Ferdinand-Brücke, turn left onto Menzingerstrasse. Cross the road and take a narrow right turn up Kuglmüllerstrasse immediately after the tiny Nymphenburg canal.

❸ Continue up Winthirstrasse past some of the grand mansions of this leafy, exclusive residential area until you reach the canal.

❻ The vast palace was constructed by five consecutive generations of Bavarian royalty, and contains several museums and galleries. The Porcelain Museum here provides a history of the famous porcelain factory (▷ 90).

❹ Turn left and stroll along the banks of the canal, along the Südliche Auffahrtsallee. During very cold winters, locals can be seen ice-skating on the canal.

❺ Eventually you will reach Schloss Nymphenburg (▷ 84–85).

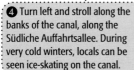

Shopping

L'ANTIPASTO

lantipasto.de

This thriving business, founded by two Italian brothers in the 1980s, stays open till late for wine tastings with antipasti, while selling quality food produce (fresh pasta, sauces, etc) during the day.

➕ F5 ✉ Sanstrasse 33 ☎ 5230 0824 🚇 U-Bahn Stiglmaierplatz

EILLES

eilles-tee.de

Originally purveyors of fine teas to Ludwig II and the Bavarian royal household, this small fragrant store also sells coffees, chocolates, biscuits, jams and wine. Shop here for gourmet gifts.

➕ E5 ✉ Donnersberger Strasse 5 ☎ 16 15 35 🚇 U-Bahn Rotkreuzplatz

ESPRESSO & BARISTA

listino-prezzi.com

Espresso & Barista is a café-cum-shop specializing in everything to do with coffee: you will find cups, coffee mills, machines, coffee-table books (about coffee), even practical courses.

➕ E5 ✉ Schlörstrasse 11 ☎ 1678 3878 🚇 U-Bahn Rotkreuzplatz

KARSTADT

karstadt.de

This central branch of the well-known German department store has everything from clothing and sportswear to toys, perfumes and electrical goods. Don't leave before checking out the roof-top terrace restaurant.

➕ H7 ✉ Bahnhofplatz ☎ 55120 🚇 U- or S-Bahn Hauptbahnhof

KRISTINA SACK

kristina-sack.de

Shopping for kitchenware was never so much fun. Kristina Sack's eclectic selection of equipment includes brightly painted crockery, tableware, soufflé molds, gadgets and party kitsch.

➕ E6 ✉ Wilderich-Lang-Strasse 6 ☎ 502 3464 🚋 Tram 16, 17

OLYMPIA EINKAUFSZENTRUM

olympia-einkaufszentrum.de

Better known to locals by the German abbreviation OEZ, Bavaria's largest shopping center is an integral part of the Olympia Park. There are more than 130 outlets here, including a selection of cafés and restaurants.

➕ E1 ✉ Hanauer Strasse 68 ☎ 1433 2910 🚇 U-Bahn Olympia Einkaufszentrum

PORZELLAN MANUFAKTUR NYMPHENBURG

nymphenburg.com

This factory once created porcelain for the royal family and it still turns out beautiful traditional designs. What you may not know is that the factory also produces exquisite porcelain hair pins, brooches, medallions and so on, once known as "gallantries," which were exchanged as presents. There is another outlet at Odeonsplatz (▷ 56).

➕ C4 ✉ Nördliches Schlossrondell 8 ☎ 179 1970 🕐 Mon–Fri 10–5 🚋 Tram 17

HANDCRAFTED PORCELAIN

The manufacture of exquisite porcelain figurines and dishes was started in 1747 by Prince Elector Maximilian III Joseph at his Nymphenburg Palace (▷ 84–85) in suburban Munich. Today about 85 artists and artisans keep alive traditional methods at a cramped factory across from the palace, throwing, forming and painting each piece by hand. Their delicate creations range from bowls and cups to graceful dancers and animals.

Entertainment and Nightlife

CAFÉ AM BEETHOVENPLATZ

mariandl.com

Munich's oldest concert-café is decorated in the belle epoque style of a Viennese coffeehouse and has a Bavarian-style beer garden. Artists, writers and musicians have enjoyed the atmosphere here since the early 1900s.

🏠 G8 ✉ Goethestrasse 51 ☎ 552 9100 ⏰ Daily 9am–1am 🚇 U-Bahn Goetheplatz 🚌 58

CIRCUS KRONE

circus-krone.com

Munich's internationally acclaimed circus is still going strong after nearly a century. It boasts Europe's largest circus auditorium, seating 3,000, and stages winter and summer programs. The shows combine traditional circus acts—clowns, animals, high-wire—with modern showbiz.

🏠 G6 ✉ Zirkus-Krone-Strasse 1-6 ☎ 545 8000 🚇 S-Bahn Hackerbrücke

MISTER B'S

misterbs.de

Enjoy your jazz in the intimate setting of this small cocktail bar. Musicians perform live from around 10pm, Thursday to Saturday.

🏠 G8 ✉ Herzog-Heinrich-Strasse 38 ☎ 53 49 01 ⏰ Tue–Sun 8pm–3am 🚇 U-Bahn Goetheplatz

NACHTGALERIE

nachtgalerie.de

Head to this former warehouse for a fun night out, dancing till dawn to chart hits. Concerts start at 10.30pm and there is an entry charge (€10)—drinks, though, are surprisingly cheap.

🏠 D7 ✉ Landsberger Strasse 185 ☎ 3455 5952 ⏰ Fri–Sat 10.30pm–4am 🚇 S-Bahn Donnersbergerbrücke 🚋 Tram 18, 19

OLYMPIA-EISSTADION

olympiapark.de

The Olympic Ice Stadium is the venue for the professional ice-hockey team, Red Bull Munich—see the website for the match calendar. Next door is a public rink where you can rent skates.

🏠 G2 ✉ Olympiapark ☎ 30670 🚇 U-Bahn Olympiazentrum

RIVER TRIP

isarflossfahrten.biz

For one of Bavaria's most enjoyable experiences, take a *Gaudiflossenfahrt*: a pleasure raft trip on the River Isar from Wolfratshausen to Thalkirchen. You will drift downstream in a convoy to the music of a brass band and a steady flow of beer from the barrels on board.

🏠 G7 ✉ Bahnhofplatz 2 ☎ 1308 5890 🚇 U- or S-Bahn Hauptbahnhof

SUMMER FESTIVAL

olympiapark.de

From late July to mid-August the Olympia Park hosts the Impark Festival. There is fun for all the family here—everything from firework displays, live music and food stalls to a funfair and giant cinema screen by the lake.

🏠 G2 ✉ Olympiapark ☎ 30670 🚇 U-Bahn Olympiazentrum

OUTDOOR MUNICH

The Englischer Garten (English Garden, ▷ 64–65) is a popular place for Munich's city dwellers to walk, cycle or sunbathe. This extensive green space stretches all the way from the middle of the city along the banks of the River Isar. The Olympiapark (▷ 82–83), the stadium site of the 1972 Olympic Games, has been converted into a park with facilities including swimming, tennis and ice-skating.

Where to Eat

AUGUSTINER-KELLER (€)

augustinerkeller.de

In the barrel-vaulted hall of the Augustiner-Keller, with its decorative hunting trophies and wood paneling, customers are seated at long tables and served Bavarian sausages and roast meats. The huge beer garden seats over 5,000 and you will hear a bell ring each time a barrel of Augustiner is opened.

➕ G6　✉ Arnulfstrasse 52　☎ 59 43 93
🕐 11.30am–1am　🚇 S-Bahn Hackerbrücke
🚋 Tram 16, 17

CAFÉ RUFFINI (€)

ruffini.de

This café-cum-konditorei is a perfect stopover for breakfast, whether you are after ham and eggs or more in the mood for cakes, croissants and freshly baked bread. Later on in the day you may also be tempted to try one of the 30 Italian wines on offer or the grappas.

➕ E4　✉ Orffstrasse 22–24　☎ 16 11 60　🕐 Tue–Sun 10am–12am　🚇 U-Bahn Rotkreuzplatz

LÖWENBRÄUKELLER (€)

loewenbraeukeller.com

Waiting staff in regional costume set the tone in this traditional Bavarian brewery restaurant. Fill up on regional dishes like *Obatzda* (a soft cheese), *Hendle* (crispy roast chicken) and *Flammkuchen* (a type of German pizza). There is a grill in the large beer garden where you can enjoy lunch under the shady trees.

➕ G6　✉ Nymphenburger Strasse 2
☎ 52 60 21　🕐 Daily 10am–12am
🚇 U-Bahn Stiglmaierplatz　🚋 Tram 20, 21

ROMANS (€€–€€€}

romans.meinlieblingsitaliener.de

Head chef, Riccardo Iannuzzi, shows a real flare in his beautifully prepared modern Italian creations. The antipasti are particularly mouthwatering.

➕ E4　✉ Romanstrasse 1　☎ 168 9898　🕐 Daily 11am–12am　🚇 U-Bahn Rotkreuzplatz

SARCLETTI (€)

sarcletti.de

Scarcletti boasts the largest ice-cream menu in town, with more than 100 flavors, from the classic pistachio to the more exotic rhubarb or butter caramel.

➕ E5　✉ Nymphenburger Strasse 155　☎ 15 53 14　🚇 U-Bahn Rotkreuzplatz

SCHLOSSCAFÉ IM PALMENHAUS (€–€€)

palmenhaus.de

This elegant café in the Nymphenburg Palace's giant palm house serves a small selection of Austrian-inspired dishes and also a selection of *torten* (cakes).

➕ B4　✉ Schloss Nymphenburg　☎ 17 53 09　🕐 Tue–Fri 11–6, Sat–Sun 10–6　🚋 51; tram 12, 16, 17

Farther Afield

There is even more to see outside of Munich's city center. Bavaria has many attractions, including several beautiful palaces, such as King Ludwig's fairy-tale castle, Neuschwanstein.

Röhrmoos

Haimhausen

Freising

Hallbergmoos

Eching

Neufahrn bei Freising

Unter-schleissheim

Ober-schleissheim

Dachau

Garching bei München

Schleissheim

Flugwerft Schleissheim

Karlsfeld

FELD-MOCHING

Speichersee

Allianz Arena

Ismaning

HARTHOF

FASANERIE-NORD

Pliening

Kirchheim bei Müchen

MOOSACH

Unterföhring

MENZING

NYMPHEN-BURG

SCHWABING

OBER-FÖHRING

DAGLFING

Feldkirchen

UAUBING

MÜNCHEN

BOGENHAUSEN

EIHAM

PASING

LAIM

KIRCH-TRUDERING

äfelfing

Zum Flaucher

BERG AM LAIM

Vaterstetten

FÜRSTEN-RIED

THAL-KIRCHEN

GIESING

RAMERS-DORF

WALD-TRUDERING

Hanegg

FORSTEN-RIED SOLLN

Tierpark Hellabrunn Zoo

PERLACH

Grasbrunn

Neuried

Neubiberg

Putzbrunn

Bavaria Filmstadt

Unterhaching

Ottobrunn

Pullach im Isartal

Waldwirtschaft Grosshesselohe

Taufkirchen

Hohenbrunn

Baierbrunn

Grünwald

Siegertsbrunn

Oberhaching

Höhenkirchen

Strasslach

Brunnthal

Schäftlarn

Dingharting

Sauerlach

Aying

Icking

Egling

Wolfratshausen

Valley

Holzkirchen

Geretsried

Dietramszell

Kirchsee

Königsdorf

Waakirchen

Bavaria Filmstadt

HIGHLIGHTS

- Stunt show
- 4-D movie experience
- Model submarine for *Das Boot*

TIP

- Phone in advance to see if there is to be any TV recording during your visit, and request tickets to be part of the audience.

Glimpse behind the scenes of Europe's largest film studios, and learn the tricks of the trade. Since its renovation, Munich's take on Hollywood has more glitz and glamor than ever before.

Film studios Founded in 1919, the Bavaria Film Studios has hosted major Hollywood productions as well as home-grown films. In the early 1970s, *Cabaret* was filmed here, starring Liza Minelli and Michael York.

Famous films In the 1980s, the studios became famous for Wolfgang Petersen's movies, such as *Das Boot*, *Enemy Mine* and *The Never Ending Story*. It was at this time that the Bavaria Film Tours began, and today you can still visit the fascinating sets for all three films.

At the Bavaria Stunt Show at these film studios you can learn how dangerous stunts are staged, while the film workshop allows school groups to shoot their own movie

Film tours Tours of the film studios last 90 minutes (with an English-language tour at 1pm daily). Older children will love directing their own films, and even playing the starring role in a thriller under coaching from one of the studio's directors. Explore familiar film sets (including an entire Berlin street, and the Gaulish village from *Asterix and Obelix versus Caesar*), watch actors at work filming, and be sure to see the breathtaking stuntmen in action in the Bavaria Stunt Show (which takes place on the set of a deserted New York suburb) with all its special effects and daring tricks. There is a thrilling 4-D motion cinema, where your seats move with the action in the film. Munich also boasts more than its fair share of cinemas (over 84). Some show the films in their original language—check the cinemas' websites for details.

THE BASICS

filmstadt.de
🞤 See map ▷ 95
✉ Bavariafilmplatz 7
☎ 6499 3557
🕐 Mid-Mar to early Nov daily 9–6 (last admission 4.30pm); early Nov to mid-Mar daily 10–5pm
🚊 Tram 25
👋 Expensive
❓ Guided tours in English daily 1pm

Dachau

HIGHLIGHTS

● Schloss Dachau and Hofgarten
● Dachauer Art Gallery
● Museum
● The memorial

TIP

● For an overview of the camp, start by watching a 22-minute documentary called "The Dachau Concentration Camp," shown at 10, 11.30, 12.30, 2 and 3 in English, and at 9.30, 11, 1.30, 2.30 and 3.30 in German.

Once people visited Dachau to see the Renaissance chateau and town, until it became synonymous with the Nazi reign of terror. Today the concentration camp (KZ-Gedenkstätte) has been preserved as a memorial to those who died here.

Summer castle The picturesque little town of Dachau, with its 18th-century pastel facades and quaint cobbled streets, is set on the steep bank of the River Amper. The Renaissance castle above the town was a popular summer residence of the Munich royals. Only one wing of the original four survives; it contains a large banquet hall with one of the most exquisitely carved ceilings in Bavaria. Nearby is the Dachauer Moos, a heath area often wreathed in mists, with a delicate light that is loved by artists.

Although Dachau is home to a former concentration camp, it is also a lovely historic town that deserves to be explored in its own right

The camp Munich residents used to come to Dachau to wander its pretty streets and visit the castle. But on 22 March 1933, only 50 days after Hitler came to power, Dachau was designated as the site of the first concentration camp of the Third Reich. Although it was not one of the main extermination camps, 31,951 deaths were recorded here between 1933 and 1945. Some original buildings have been restored as a memorial, a poignant reminder of the camp's 206,000 inmates. The museum documents the camp's history and the atrocities that happened here, with the help of audio guides. There are tours in English Monday to Friday at 11am and 1pm, and from July to October, Saturday and Sunday at 12.15 (duration 150 minutes, small charge). The gates still bear the bitterly ironic *"Arbeit macht frei"* ("Work makes you free").

THE BASICS

➕ See map ▷ 95

Ⓢ S-Bahn Dachau

Concentration Camp

kz-gedenkstaette-dachau.de

✉ Alte Römerstrasse 75

☎ (08131) 752 87

🕐 Daily 9–5

🚆 S-Bahn to Dachau, then bus 726 to KZ-Gedenkstätte Haupteingang or 724 to KZ-Gedenkstätte Parkplatz

♿ Excellent

🆓 Free

Schleissheim

The Old Palace now houses collections from the Bavarian National Museum

THE BASICS

schloesser.bayern.de
➕ See map ▷ 95
✉ Max-Emanuel-Platz 1, Oberschleissheim
☎ 2429 5106
🕐 Apr–Sep Tue–Sun 9–6; Oct–Mar 10–4
🚃 S-Bahn Oberschleissheim
🚌 292
♿ Few
💷 Old Palace: inexpensive; New/Lustheim: inexpensive; combined ticket: moderate

HIGHLIGHTS

Old Palace
● Religious folk art
New Palace
● Great Gallery
Palace Lustheim
● Meissen Porcelain Museum

The three Schleissheim palaces capture the splendor of Munich's past. Make sure you see the Great Gallery, the delightful French-style gardens and the magnificent display of Meissen porcelain.

Old Palace In 1597 Duke Wilhelm V bought a farm to the east of the Dachau moor as a retirement residence. His son, Prince Elector Maximilian I, later transformed it into an Italian-style Renaissance palace, and called it the Altes Schloss Schleissheim. Today it contains part of the Bavarian National Museum, including a gallery devoted to international religious folk art.

New Palace The beautiful Neues Schloss, the Versailles of Munich, was commissioned by Prince Elector Max Emanuel II as a summer residence. The largest palace complex of its day, it demonstrated his wealth and power. Despite severe damage during World War II, the sumptuous rococo interior remains largely intact. The Great Gallery, over 60m (197ft) long, contains the Bavarian State Art Collection. One of the most remarkable collections of baroque paintings in Europe, it includes masterpieces by Rubens, Titian, Veronese and van Dyck.

Palace Lustheim Separated from the New Palace by formal gardens and encircled by a decorative canal, Palace Lustheim was planned as an island of happiness for Max Emanuel's bride Maria Antonia. It now houses Germany's largest collection of Meissen porcelain.

More to See

ALLIANZ ARENA

allianz-arena.de

Munich's stadium is home to Germany's most successful football (soccer) club—FC Bayern München. Its futuristic facade, comprising nearly 3,000 inflated translucent foil panels, has earned it the nicknames "life belt" and "rubber dinghy." The 75,000-seater stadium glows red (the club's predominant color) on match days.

⊞ See map ▷ 95 ⊠ Werner-Heisenberg-Allee 25 ☎ 6993 1222/3509 ⏰ Daily 10–6 except on home match days ⚑ Excellent Ⓤ U-Bahn Fröttmaning ❷ For games, visit online ticket shop

AMMERSEE

ammersee-region.de

Ammersee, with its lake promenades and sandy beaches, is set in lush green countryside at the heart of Munich's lake district, easily reached by S-Bahn (journey time about 50 minutes). Highlights include a trip on Bavaria's oldest paddle-steamer and Kloster Andechs (▷ 102). The lake is known for its curious phenomenon: a *Schaukelwelle* (rocking wave), which goes back and forth every 24 minutes, the water rising and falling about 10cm (4in) against the shore.

⊞ See map ▷ 94 Ⓢ S-Bahn Herrsching

FLUGWERFT SCHLEISSHEIM

deutsches-museum.de

A must for plane buffs, this is an extension of the Deutsches Museum's aviation display, featuring fixed-wing aircraft, helicopters, gliders and engines, plus museum staff undertaking restoration.

⊞ See map ▷ 95 ⊠ Effnerstrasse 18, Oberschleissheim ☎ 315 7140 ⏰ Daily 9–5 Ⓢ S-Bahn Oberschleissheim 🚌 292 💶 Moderate

FREISING

freising.de

On the left bank of the River Isar, 32km (20 miles) northeast of Munich, Freising's hilltop cathedral is the jewel in the old town's crown. Freising is also home to the

The glowing "rubber dinghy" of Allianz Arena

Sailing boats on the Ammersee

Weihenstephan brewery, the world's oldest in continuous use.
➕ See map ▷ 95 🚈 S-Bahn to Freising

KLOSTER ANDECHS

andechs.de

One of Germany's most important pilgrimage destinations, Andechs monastery is famous for its centuries-old brewing tradition and its *Andechser Bock* beer.
➕ See map ▷ 94 ✉ Bergstrasse 2, Andechs ☎ 01852 3760 🕐 Daily but various for monastery and brewery 🚈 S-Bahn Herrsching then by local bus ✋ Free

STARNBERGER SEE

sta5.de

The largest of the five lakes just south of the city, its banks still lined with the baroque palaces of Bavaria's aristocracy, remains the domain of the rich and famous. Today, the area offers horseback-riding, golf, swimming and sailing.
➕ See map ▷ 94 🚈 S-Bahn Tutzing (and earlier lakeside stations)

TIERPARK HELLABRUNN ZOO

tierpark-hellabrunn.de

The world's first Geo-Zoo with animals grouped in habitats according to their regions of origin.
➕ See map ▷ 95 ✉ Tierparkstrasse 30 ☎ 62 50 80 🕐 Apr–Sep daily 8–6; Oct–Mar daily 9–5 🚇 U-Bahn Thalkirchen 🚌 52 💶 Expensive

WALDWIRTSCHAFT GROSSHESSELOHE

waldwirtschaft.de

A long-time local beer garden haunt overlooking the Isar gorge and famous for its live jazz.
➕ See map ▷ 95 ✉ Georg-Kalb-Strasse 3 ☎ 7499 4030 🕐 Daily 11–9.30 🚈 S-Bahn Isartalbahnhof Grosshesselohe

ZUM FLAUCHER

zum-flaucher.de

A bit off the tourist track, this scenic beer garden is next to the River Isar. A great spot for an evening picnic.
➕ See map ▷ 95 ✉ Isarauen 8 ☎ 723 2677 🕐 Daily 11–10 🚇 U-Bahn Brudermühlstrasse, then short walk

Starnberger See, with the Alps in the background

Excursions

AUGSBURG

Bavaria's oldest city has a 2,000-year history and you'll find styles of all the major architectural periods. The Renaissance flourished here, and rococo became known as the Augsburg style. Augsburg is Bavaria's third largest city, and its oldest, founded in 15BC as the Roman legionary fortress Augusta Vindelicorum. The old town boasts a splendid Romanesque-Gothic cathedral, imposing city squares and 15 museums and art galleries. The Renaissance Rathaus dominates Rathausplatz; inside, the restored Goldener Saal (Golden Hall) is famous for its magnificent portals, ceiling and mural paintings. With 142 residences built in 1521 at the expense of the wealthy merchant banker Jakob Fugger, the Fuggerei are the oldest almshouses in the world. Still in use, one of the houses is open to the public, along with the World War II bunker, built for residents at the time. The Fuggerei (1514–23) are the oldest almshouses in the world. On Frauentorstrasse is Mozart House, the birthplace of Leopold Mozart, father of Wolfgang, and now a Mozart museum.

THE BASICS

augsburg-tourismus.de
Distance: 72km (45 miles)
Journey Time: 30–40 mins by train
🚉 Augsburg
🛈 Rathausplatz 1, 86150 Augsburg
☎ 0821 502 0721

BAD TÖLZ

The beautiful spa town of Bad Tölz, at the foot of the Bavarian Alps, is famous for its iodine-rich springs and peat baths. The cobbled main street, lined with pastel-colored houses ornately decorated with murals, takes the visitor past the Old Town Hall and museum, then leads up to the twin-spired Kreuzkirche noted for its Leonhard chapel. Bad Tölz is a perfect base for skiing and other mountain activities. Nearby Blombergbahn is Germany's longest summer toboggan run and the scene in winter of a crazy sled-flying competition. For the best views, take the chair lift.

THE BASICS

badtoelz.de
Distance: 40km (25 miles)
Journey Time: 1 hour by train
🚉 Hourly trains from Munich's main station
🛈 Max-Höfler-Platz 1, 83646 Bad Tölz
☎ 08041 78670

FARTHER AFIELD EXCURSIONS

CHIEMSEE

Locally called the Bavarian Sea, Chiemsee is the largest of the Bavarian lakes. Its lush scenery and picture-postcard Alpine backdrop has attracted artists for centuries and today draws visitors to its shores for swimming, sailing and other pursuits. The lake's main attraction is Herrenchiemsee, site of Ludwig II's ambitious summer palace—a replica of the French Palace of Versailles. Only the central wing of the building was completed, including the spectacular Hall of Mirrors. The smaller island of Frauenchiemsee has a fishing village and a Benedictine nunnery founded in 872, where the nuns still make a special liqueur, called *Klosterlikör,* from an ancient recipe. A useful and picturesque base for exploring the area is the market town of Prien am Chiemsee which is also famous as a health resort.

THE BASICS

chiemsee-alpenland.de
herren-chiemsee.de
chiemsee-schiffahrt.de
Distance: 80km (50 miles)
Journey Time: 1 hour
by train then 30-min walk
to ferry
🚆 Frequent trains to Prien
from Munich's main station
ℹ️ Chiemsee-Infocenter,
Felden 10, 83233 Bernau
am Chiemsee
☎ 08051 96 55 50 and
08051 6090 (ferry)
🕐 Guided palace tours
9–5 (summer), 9.40–3.30
(winter)

SCHLOSS LINDERHOF

Set among magnificent mountain scenery and surrounded by forest, Ludwig II's Schloss Linderhof began as a hunting lodge belonging to his father, Maximilian II, and was based on the Petit Trianon at Versailles. Completed in 1878, the lavish interiors, all decorated in eccentrically opulent pseudo- Renaissance and baroque styles, include a hall of mirrors and an enormous chandelier weighing 500kg (1,000lb). Ludwig used the palace as a retreat and rarely received visitors here. The formal French gardens, fanciful fountains, grotto and follies are a wonderful place to explore. The highlight—an exotic Moorish kiosk with a peacock throne—recently restored was acquired by Ludwig from the World Exhibition in Paris in 1876 and the timber-framed Gurnemanz Hermitage, inspired by a scene in Wagner's opera, Parsifal.

THE BASICS

linderhof.de
Distance: 100km
(62 miles)
Journey Time: 2.25
hours
🚆 Train to
Oberammergau, then
bus 9622
✉️ Linderhof 12, 82488
Ettal
☎ 08822 92030
🕐 Guided palace tours
Apr–Sep daily 9 6; Oct–
Mar 10–4
💰 Moderate

THE BASICS

neuschwanstein.de
Distance: 120km
(75 miles)
Journey Time: About 2
hours by train then bus 73
to Hohenschwangau and
walk uphill
🚉 Füssen
☎ 08362 930830
🕐 Guided tours Apr–Sep
daily 9–6; Oct–Mar 10–3.
Online reservation pos-
sible with credit card and
48-hr advance warning
🚌 Organised coach trips
frequently available
💰 Expensive
ℹ Tourist Information
Schwangau, Münchener
Strasse 2, 87645
Schwangau

SCHLOSS NEUSCHWANSTEIN

This fairy-tale castle is a magical white-turreted
affair nestled in a pine forest in the foothills of
the Bavarian Alps. In an attempt to make the
fantasy world of Wagnerian opera a reality,
"Mad" King Ludwig II commissioned a stage
designer rather than an architect to design this
romantic, theatrical castle, and watched it being
built by telescope from his father's neighboring
castle of Hohenschwangau.

Neuschwanstein is the most photographed
building in Germany, and the inspiration for
Disney's Sleeping Beauty Castle at Disneyland
following a visit by Walt Disney and his wife in
the 1950s. Sadly only 15 of the 65 rooms were
finished and Ludwig spent just a few days here
before he was dethroned in 1886. The lavish
interior is worth lining up for, with its extravagant decor and vast wall paintings of Wagnerian
scenes. Since childhood, Ludwig had a passion
for German legend as epitomized in the operas
of Richard Wagner. Following a performance of
Lohengrin, Ludwig became an enthusiastic
admirer and patron of Wagner.

Together with Herrenchiemsee (▷ 105) and
Linderhof (▷ 105), King Ludwig II's extravagant
fairy-tale castles were a drain on the regency's
treasury. As state affairs became increasingly
neglected, the doomed monarch was declared
insane on June 10 and, just a few days later
on June 13, 1886, met a mysterious watery
death on the eastern shore of the Starnberger
See (▷ 102).

Fortunately, Ludwig's request to destroy
Neuschwanstein on his death was ignored. Just
seven weeks after his death, the castle was
opened to the public to pay off the enormous
debts he had incurred building it. Today, the
castle is the most popular and profitable tourist
attraction in Bavaria.

Where to Stay

Munich has its quota of luxury hotels, but it also offers authentic Bavarian accommodations, and some excellent youth hostels and camping options for those on a tight budget.

Introduction

There are more than 40,000 hotel beds in Munich. Budget accommodations are relatively easy to find; double rooms are better value than singles. If you are visiting in low season (November to March) you will probably be spoiled for choice—unless a large trade fair is taking place. The *Oktoberfest* (late September to early October) is a busy time, so you will need to reserve somewhere as much as a year in advance. The best advice is to always reserve ahead.

Types of Hotels

Munich has its share of well-known hotel chains, but there are still many that are family-owned. Smaller, privately owned hotels sometimes do not have any rooms designated as non-smoking, so check when you book. Air-conditioning is not standard in Munich hotels, particularly those in historic buildings, and a few may not have an elevator. A large breakfast buffet is normally included in the price in mid-range hotels. Some smaller hotels and pensions do not accept credit cards. The Upper Bavarian countryside south of Munich is also geared to welcoming tourists, so you may consider staying there and commuting into the city by S-Bahn, train or bus.

Star Ratings

Most hotels in Germany are assigned a star rating from one to five, and prices usually reflect this. However, bear in mind that higher prices are not necessarily a guarantee of quality. For this reason, it's always a good idea to ask to see a room before booking, or if you're making a reservation online, look at any pictures.

JUGENDHERBERGEN

The Germans are mad about hostels ("Jugendherbergen") and hosteling. Facilities are generally good, but some hostels require visitors to vacate the building during the day, and others have a curfew (although this is usually sensibly late). For reservations and further information, visit djh-ris.de, which has an English version.

Budget Hotels

ACANTHUS

acanthushotel.de

Excellent for access to the inner-city sights as well as the *Oktoberfest* grounds, all rooms are spotless and have a flatscreen TV and free Internet. Book the Junior Suite and you will have lovely views of the Munich skyline. A generous breakfast is served until late.

✚ H8 ✉ An der Hauptfeuerwache 14
☎ 23 18 80 Ⓢ Sendlinger Tor

AURBACHER

hotel-aurbacher.de

The modern exterior belies this hotel's secret—a lovely garden and breakfast room. For direct access to the garden, book one of the prized large double rooms, partly decorated with antique furniture. The other rooms on offer are functional, if a little tired in their decor.

✚ K9 ✉ Aurbacherstrasse 5 ☎ 48 09 10
Ⓢ S-Bahn Rosenheimer Platz

BLAUER BOCK

hotelblauerbock.de

A listed building in an attractive square dating back to the 16th century, this mid-sized refurbished hotel with parking facilities is great value for its location between the Viktualienmarkt and Marienplatz. The rooms are a reasonable size for the price, and clean.

✚ J7 ✉ Sebastiansplatz 9 ☎ 23 17 80
Ⓢ U- or S-Bahn Marienplatz

FLEMING'S CITY

flemings-hotels.com

This smart central four-star hotel prides itself on its modern yet intimate atmosphere. Facilities include stylish rooms, all with free internet connections, a popular brasserie-cum-wine-bar, and a small fitness area.

✚ H7 ✉ Bayerstrasse 47 ☎ 4444 660
Ⓢ S-Bahn Karlsplatz

GÄSTEHAUS ENGLISCHER GARTEN

hotelenglischergarten.de

This little gem of a guest house in a restored ivy-clad building has a tranquil location by the Isar River and opposite the Seehaus restaurant and the nearby beer garden. The rooms are quaint and clean, if a little old-fashioned, and note that there are only 12 rooms in the main building and 13 in the annex.

✚ K4 ✉ Liebergesellstrasse 8 ☎ 383 9410
Ⓢ U-Bahn Münchner Freiheit

DAS HOTEL IN MÜNCHEN

das-hotel-in-muenchen.de

This Schwabing hotel occupies an elegant town house dating from 1902, when the area was first developed. Each room has its own color scheme and some have period features like ceiling moldings and small balconies. Visitors who enjoy art will appreciate its proximity to the Pinakothek galleries.

✚ J5 ✉ Türkenstrasse 35 ☎ 288 1400
Ⓢ U-Bahn Universität

CAMPING

For really cheap accommodations in Munich, why not bring a tent? There are many campsites in and around Munich. The best, and the most central, is Camping Thalkirchen (☎ 723 1707; muenchen.de), attractively positioned along the River Isar, with 700 places open from mid-March until the end of October. There is no need to reserve except during the *Oktoberfest*.

Mid-Range Hotels

ANNA

annahotel.de

Design and ambience are the watchwords at this mid-sized hotel with minimalist decor, large bright rooms and a clever interplay of light and color. The five "tower rooms" have views of Karlsplatz Stachus. Anna is excellent value in low season.

➕ H7 ✉ Schützenstrasse 1 ☎ 59 99 40 🚇 U- or S-Bahn Hauptbahnhof

CARLTON

carlton-astoria.de

This is an unpretentious but comfortable hotel in an ideal location if you are planning to spend a lot of time in the art museums of the Maxvorstadt. Staff are friendly and helpful and the buffet breakfast is a cut above the norm.

➕ J6 ✉ Fürstenstrasse 12 ☎ 3839 630 🚇 U-Bahn Odeonsplatz

EXQUISIT

hotel-exquisit.com

Ideally placed for the *Oktoberfest* grounds as well as downtown sights, this family-run hotel has decent-sized rooms as well as a bar and restaurant. After a long day, the sauna is a plus.

➕ H7 ✉ Pettenkoferstrasse 3 ☎ 551 990 🚇 U-Bahn Sendlinger Tor

H'OTELLO

hotello.de

One of a number of well-designed hotels springing up in the city, H'Otello abounds with minimalist elegance. All the rooms are doubles and equipped with smart technology for your amusement. An alternative source of entertainment is the cocktail bar.

➕ J8 ✉ Baaderstrasse 1 ☎ 4583 1200 🚇 S-Bahn Isartor

INSEL MÜHLE

inselmuehle-muenchen.com

This beautifully renovated and timbered 15th-century corn mill has tastefully decorated rooms as well as its own beer garden and restaurant. It lies just outside the city (3.7 miles/6km from the Nymphenburg Palace) and is well worth the extra trip.

➕ Off map to west ✉ Von-Kahr-Strasse 87 ☎ 81010 🚇 S-Bahn Allach

LA MAISON

hotel-la-maison

Playing up to its location in Bohemian Schwabing, this chic hotel has good-sized room with subdued decor. Breakfast is from a menu, not self-service.

➕ K4 ✉ Occamstrasse 24 ☎ 3303 5550 🚇 U-Bahn Münchner Freiheit

MARIANDL

hotelmariandl.de

Take a step back into the past and stay in this turreted town house from the belle epoque era (c1900). The generously sized rooms are furnished in period style, some with antiques

(though a few are without bathrooms). Guests have access to the music café Am Beethovenplatz (▷ 91) on the ground floor.

➕ G8 ✉ Goethestrasse 51 ☎ 552 9100
🚇 U-Bahn Goetheplatz 🚌 58

OPERA

hotel-opera.de

This small hotel is in an exquisite Jugendstil mansion. All of the rooms are immaculate and quirkily furnished in a variety of styles. Breakfast is served in sumptuous surroundings.

➕ K7 ✉ St-Anna-Strasse 10 ☎ 210 4940
🚇 U- or S-Bahn Marienplatz

PENSION SEIBEL

seibel-hotels-munich.de

This pension has bags of charm, with traditional Bavarian decoration in the rooms and breakfast room. The location is great too–just behind the Viktualienmarkt (▷ 33). Book early for lower rates or stay in low season.

➕ J8 ✉ Reichenbachstrasse 8 ☎ 2319 180
🚊 Tram 17, 18

PLATZL

platzl.de

A friendly hotel with 167 rooms, tastefully decorated if a little on the small side. The amenities include a fitness area, a restaurant in a converted mill and the Wirtshaus Aying, a rustic-style inn with patio seating in summer.

➕ J7 ✉ Sparkassenstrasse 10 ☎ 23 70 30
🚇 U- or S-Bahn Marienplatz

RUBY LILLY

ruby-hotels.com/muenchen

A reminder that Munich is a city of design, the rooms in this decidedly hip hotel are furnished in minimalist style. You are guaranteed to get a good night's sleep as all rooms are specially soundproofed, have dimmer switches, large beds and hypo-allergenic bed linen. Relax in the cozy library, the rock 'n' roll themed café bar or on the roof-top terrace.

➕ G6 ✉ Dachauer Strasse 37 ☎ 9545 7082
🚇 U-Bahn Königsplatz

SPLENDID-DOLLMANN

hotel-splendid-dollmann.de

A small centrally located hotel in a listed building dating from the 19th century, the Dollmann has airy and ample-sized rooms, decorated in a range of styles including baroque, Louis XIV and Bavarian.

➕ K7 ✉ Thierschstrasse 49 ☎ 23 80 80
🚇 U-Bahn Lehel

TORBRÄU

torbraeu.de

This friendly hotel near the Isartor is the oldest in Munich, founded in 1490 and run by the same family for the last 100 years. Former guests include the composers Mendelssohn and Liszt, the poet Heinrich Heine and writer Hans Christian Andersen. The restaurant and piano bar, Schapeau, is worth investigating, and it hosts a "swing brunch" on Sundays.

➕ J7 ✉ Tal 41 ☎ 24 23 40 🚇 S-Bahn Isator

PRICES

Like any metropolis, Munich can proudly claim a clutch of first-class hotels of worldwide reputation, but most of the city's 350-plus establishments are in the medium to lower price ranges. Except, that is, when a major trade fair or the *Oktoberfest* beer festival takes place, when prices can increase substantially.

Luxury Hotels

PRICES
Expect to pay over €250 per night for a luxury hotel.

BAYERISCHER HOF

bayerischerhof.de

This rather grand hotel vies with the Four Seasons in the history and traditions stakes, as it dates from 1841 and guests can still occupy the suite decorated to please King Ludwig I. There are panoramic views across Munich from the Blue Spa, with its swimming pool and roof garden. The Atelier restaurant has two Michelin stars.

➕ H7 ✉ Promenadeplatz 2–6 ☎ 21200 🚇 U- or S-Bahn Marienplatz ♿ 3 rooms adapted for disabled access

HILTON MUNICH PARK

3.hilton.com

The main reason for choosing the Hilton Park must be for the views over the Englischer Garten. Like the hotel itself, the rooms have a sleek modern look and the facilities are what you would expect for accommodations in this price range, including outdoor dining spaces, a pool and a business area.

➕ K6 ✉ Am Tucherpark 7 ☎ 38450 🚇 54, 154; tram 17

KEMPINSKI HOTEL VIER JAHRESZEITEN

kempinski-vierjahreszeiten.com

The elegant, traditional Four Seasons Hotel was established in the mid-19th century as a guesthouse for royalty visiting Maximilian II. The facilities include a fitness center, sauna, spa and swimming pool, and the recently opened Schwarzreiter restaurant is gaining in reputation for its subtle Young Bavarian cuisine.

➕ J7 ✉ Maximilianstrasse 17 ☎ 21250 🚇 U-Bahn Odeonsplatz 🚊 Tram 19

KÖNIGSHOF

koenigshof-hotel.de

In the capable hands of the Geisel family since 1938, the small, luxury hotel with well-appointed rooms prides itself on its personalized service, with each guest addressed by name. The gourmet restaurant has been awarded a Michelin star.

➕ H7 ✉ Karlsplatz 25 ☎ 55 13 60 🚇 U- or S-Bahn Karlsplatz

MANDARIN ORIENTAL

mandarinoriental.com

The Munich hotel where you are most likely to rub shoulders with international celebrities—previous guests have included Prince Charles, Madonna, Bill Gates and the England soccer squad. The Matsuhisa restaurant has received accolades for its exotic Japanese-Peruvian cuisine. A typical room overlooks the Hofbräuhaus and the historic old town and is decorated with artwork and cherrywood furniture. Another plus is the fitness center, open 24 hours a day.

➕ J7 ✉ Neuturmstrasse 1 ☎ 29 09 80 🚇 U- or S-Bahn Marienplatz

LE MERIDIEN

lemeridienmunich.com

This relative newcomer to the scene has an unrivaled central location for easy access to the city's museums, theaters and fashion boutiques. The hotel combines old-world charm with state-of-the-art amenities in its spacious rooms and suites, along with a soothing spa to re-invigorate guests.

➕ H7 ✉ Bayerstrasse 41 ☎ 24220 🚇 U- or S-Bahn Hauptbahnhof

Need to Know

Everything you need to know to make your visit to Munich a success, from the initial planning stages through to practical tips on the ground.

Planning Ahead

When to Go

Munich is busiest between April and September when the weather is at its best. May is the start of the beer garden season, while in summer the city is popular for its opera festival and lively park life. Fall draws beer-lovers to the *Oktoberfest* (▷ 92) and December is crowded with shoppers who come for the Christmas market.

> **TIME**
>
> Munich is one hour ahead of the UK, six hours ahead of New York and nine hours ahead of Los Angeles.

AVERAGE DAILY MAXIMUM TEMPERATURES

JAN	FEB	MAR	APR	MAY	JUN	JUL	AUG	SEP	OCT	NOV	DEC
34°F	34°F	46°F	57°F	64°F	69°F	76°F	74°F	75°F	67°F	57°F	38°F
1°C	1°C	8°C	14°C	18°C	21°C	24°C	23°C	24°C	19°C	14°C	3°C

Spring (March to May) is at its most delightful in May, with mild days and the least rainfall.

Summer (June to August) is the sunniest season, with blue skies and long, hazy days, but also the occasional thunderstorm.

Fall (September to November) is often still warm and sunny—the so-called *Altweibersommer* ("old wives summer").

Winter (December to February) is the coldest time of year, with frequent snowfalls.

WHAT'S ON

February *Fasching:* High-point of the carnival season, which begins in Nov.

March *Starkbierzeit:* Strong beer season.

April *Spring Festival:* A two-week mini *Oktoberfest* at the Theresienwiese.
Ballet Festival Week.
Auer Mai Dult: First of three annual fairs and flea markets.

May *May Day* (May 1): Traditional maypole dancing at the Viktualienmarkt.
Maibockzeit: A season of special strong lagers originating from North Germany.
Corpus Christi (second Thu after Whitsun): A magnificent Catholic procession dating back to 1343.
Spargelzeit: Celebrates the many ways there are to serve asparagus.

June *Founding of Munich* (Jun 14): From Marienplatz to Odeonsplatz the streets fill with music, street performances and refreshment stalls.
Film Festival: A week of international cinematic art.
Tollwood Festival: The Olympiapark hosts an alternative festival of rock, jazz, cabaret, food and folklore.

July *Opera Festival:* The climax of the cultural year.
Auer Jacobi Dult: The second annual Dult.
Kocherlball: A traditional workers' ball at 6am in the Englischer Garten.

August *Summer Festival:* Two weeks of fireworks and festivities in Olympiapark.

September *Oktoberfest:* The world's largest beer festival.

October *Auer Kirchweih Dult:* The third annual Dult.
German Art and Antiques Fair.

December *Christkindlmarkt:* Christmas market.

NEED TO KNOW PLANNING AHEAD

Munich Online

muenchen.de
This is the official Munich Tourist Office website, including online hotel reservations and general information on the local weather, city sights, guided tours, shopping, restaurants, nightlife and special events.

munichfound.de
The monthly English-language magazine *Munich Found* caters to visitors and residents alike with tips on local events, a comprehensive city guide and restaurant and nightlife listings, as well as children's sports and activities.

munich-partyearth.com
Up-to-date information on Munich's nightlife scene with details of all the latest concerts, bars and clubs. A must for party animals.

schloesser.bayern.de
A comprehensive and informative guide to the palaces, castles, fortresses, residences, parks, gardens and lakes in Munich and throughout Bavaria.

museen-in-bayern.de
Detailed site covering 50 museums in Munich alone, as well as in the surrounding region.

travelforkids.com/Funtodo/Germany/munich.htm
Brief descriptions of attractions for children and families in and around Munich.

mvv-muenchen.de/en
Everything you could wish to know about the Munich transport system, with maps, electronic timetables, tickets and prices for the city's S-Bahn (urban rail), U-Bahn (underground), trams and buses.

biergarten.com
A comprehensive guide (in German only) to the best of Munich's beer gardens.

TRAVEL SITES

munich-airport.de
For details of flight arrivals and departures, general travel information, airport facilities and transport links with the city.

fodors.com
A complete travel planning site. You can research prices and weather; book air tickets, cars and rooms; pose questions to fellow travelers and find links to other useful sites.

INTERNET CAFÉS

Coffee Fellows
coffee-fellows.de
✉ Leopoldstrasse 70
☎ 3889 8470
🕐 7am–midnight
📶 Free WLAN

Black Bean
black-bean.de/muenchner-freiheit
✉ Muenchner Freiheit 12
☎ 3301 9869 🕐 Daily 7am–9pm 📶 Free

WLAN
WLAN is a free Internet service offered by the city. The Internet can be accessed in many cafés, restaurants and hotels, but also in the following public areas: Marienplatz, Sendlinger Tor, Odeonsplatz and Stachus.

Getting There

ENTRY

For the latest passport and visa information, check your relevant embassy website (UK: gov.uk; USA: usembassy.gov).

TOURIST OFFICES

munich-tourist.de
● **Hauptbahnhof**
✉ Bahnhofplatz 2
☎ 2339 6500
🕐 Mon–Sat 9–8, Sun 10–6;
● **Head Office (adminis-tration only)**
Tourismusamt München
✉ Sendlinger Strasse 1, 80331 München
🕐 Mon–Fri 10–8, Sat 10–4
● **Neues Rathaus**
✉ Marienplatz 2
🕐 Mon–Fri 9–7, Sat 9–4

German National Tourist Offices
germany.travel
● **UK** ✉ 60 Buckingham Palace Rd, London SW1W OAH ☎ 020 7317 0910
● **US** ✉ 122 East 42nd Street, Suite 2000, New York, NY 10168–0072
☎ (212) 661 7200
● **Australia** ✉ Gate 7, 32 Crown St, Woolloomooloo NSW 2001 ☎ 02 9356 2945
● **Canada** ✉ 2 Bloor Street West, Suite 2601, Toronto, Ontario M4W 3E2
☎ (416) 935 1896

AIRPORTS

Munich's international airport, Flughafen München Franz-Josef-Strauss, is located 28km (17.5 miles) north of the city, and offers services to over 150 destinations worldwide. Facilities include a bank, pharmacy and a medical facility, as well as a variety of shops, restaurants and cafés.

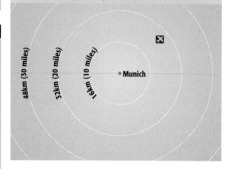

48km (30 miles) · 32km (20 miles) · 16km (10 miles) · **Munich**

ARRIVING AT FLUGHAFEN MÜNCHEN FRANZ-JOSEF-STRAUSS

The S-Bahn (urban train network) offers two services to the city from platforms located beneath the airport's main shopping area. S-Bahn 8 runs every 10 minutes from 4am until 1.02am, while S-Bahn 1 runs every 20 minutes from 5.50am until 12.10am, and also Monday to Friday at 4.30am and weekends at 5.30am. Tickets should be purchased from the machines in the shopping area before going down to the platform. Remember to stamp your ticket in the blue punch-machine *(Entwerter)* on the platform to validate it before boarding the train (unpunched tickets can incur a fine). A single journey to the heart of the city costs €11.00. Alternatively, an airport bus leaves Munich North Terminal every 15 min-utes from 6.20am to 9.40pm, taking 45 minutes to reach the main railway station. A sin-gle ticket costs €10.50.

ARRIVING BY BUS

There are frequent coach links with other German cities, starting from the main bus terminal beside the main railway station.

ARRIVING BY TRAIN

Trains take around 18 hours to Munich from Calais, in France, or Ostend, in Belgium. Munich has good connections with most major European cities. Most trains terminate at the main station (Hauptbahnhof). The east station (Ostbahnhof) takes regular motorail services from other German stations and from Paris, Budapest, Athens, Istanbul and Rimini. Train information from German Railways (Deutsche Bahn) is available in the main station's Travel Centre *(Reisezentrum,* call 1806 99 66 33).

ARRIVING BY CAR

Munich is well served by motorways (highways) and a ring road provides easy access to the city. Follow the clearly marked speed restrictions. Fines are harsh. Strect parking is difficult in the heart of the city. Car parks charge around €20 a day. Try the Mühoga Münchner Hochgaragen (Adolf-Kolping-Strasse 10) or the Tiefgarage von der Opera (Max-Joseph-Platz 4).
● Car rental: Avis, avis.de; Airport: 9759 7600, Hauptbahnhof: 550 2251

CONSULATES
● UK at Möhlstrasse 5, call 21 10 90
● US at Königinstrasse 5, call 28880
● Canada at Tal 29, call 219 9570

Getting Around

DISCOUNTS

● Children under six travel free and aged six to 14 at reduced fares.
● The City Tourcard, available from tourist offices and S- and U-Bahn stations gives unlimited travel for 24 hours on all public transport plus savings of up to 50 percent on admission to major city attractions including museums, city tours, bicycle rentals and the zoo. The price ranges from €11.00 for one person to €29.10 for a group day ticket (mvv-muenchen.de).

VISITORS WITH DISABILITIES

Access for visitors with disabilities is generally good in Munich, although some older attractions have few facilities. The Tourist Office's brochure *Munich for Physically Challenged Tourists* (in German) contains useful information on travel, lodgings, restaurants, arts and culture, city tours and leisure, and the MVV publishes a map detailing transport facilities.
For more information contact the Städtischer Beraterkreis Behinderte Geschäftsstelle (central advice bureau for people with disabilities): bb-m.info ✉ Burgstrasse 4 ☎ 2332 4452.

GETTING AROUND

Munich has an excellent, albeit complicated, public transport network, with two urban railways (S-Bahn rapid transit and U-Bahn subway), and a comprehensive network of bus and tram routes.

The local transport authority is the Münchner Verkehrs- und Tarifverbund (MVV) at Thierschstrasse 2 (tel 4142 4344).

U-Bahn and S-Bahn provide a regular service within 40km (25 miles) of central Munich. Routes are referred to by their final stop. Underground trains run every 5 or 10 minutes from about 5am to 1am (later on weekends). Tickets are available from automatic ticket machines at stations, MVV sales points in many stations, or in newspaper shops. Before boarding a train, you must put your ticket in the blue punching machine *(Entwerter)*.

On buses and trams you must stamp your ticket upon boarding. Single tickets can be bought from the driver (with small change only). Multiple tickets, also valid for U- and S-Bahn, can be bought from vending machines at train stations, but not from the driver. Some trams have ticket vending machines on board. Bus and tram routes are numbered and the vehicle has a destination board showing where it is going.

Two late-night bus lines run Monday to Friday and six lines on Saturday and Sunday. Four tram lines operate between the heart of the city and the suburbs once an hour from 1.30am to 4.30am.

TYPES OF TICKET

● The MVV network is divided into fare zones. Prices are based on the number of zones required to complete the trip. For most sightseeing you will remain in the *Innenraum* (interior area—marked blue on station maps). To travel farther you need a ticket valid for the *Gesamtnetz* (total network).
● Traveling without a valid ticket can result in a heavy fine.

- *Kurzstrecke*: short-trip single tickets can be bought for journeys covering only four stops; two may be U- or S-Bahn stops. A trip must not last more than one hour and can only be used in one direction. Unlimited transfers are permitted.
- *Streifenkarte*: a strip of tickets. For each journey, stamp the appropriate number of strips. A short trip is one strip. More than two U- or S-Bahn stops within one zone is two strips. If you are traveling outside the blue *Innenraum* zone, a notice shows how many strips you need to punch.
- *Einzelfahrkarte*: single tickets can be bought covering any number of zones, but a *Streifenkarte* usually works out cheaper.
- *Tageskarte*: one day's unlimited travel from 9am until 6am the following day. Purchase either a *Single-Tageskarte* for one person, or a *Gruppen-Tageskarte* for up to five people (maximum two adults).
- *Isarcard*: a weekly or monthly ticket providing unlimited travel on MVV transport, available at MVV ticket offices or ticket vending machines.

THE U- AND S-BAHN
- Smoking is banned on trains and in stations.
- Bicycles may be taken on the trains all day Saturday, Sunday and public holidays; on weekdays not at rush hour (6–9am, 4–6pm).

TRAMS
- Scenic routes: trams 16, 17, 18, 19, 20, 21 and 27 operate around the old town; tram 20 goes to the Englischer Garten; tram 27 is useful for exploring Schwabing.

MAPS AND TIMETABLES
- MVV station ticket offices and tourist information offices supply free maps and information.

TAXIS
- Taxis are cream-colored; stands are throughout the city. They are not particularly cheap.

WOMEN TRAVELERS

- Frauenhaus München offers 24-hour help for women, frauenhilfe-muenchen.de ☎ 35 48 30
- Munich airport and other city car parks have well-lit, reserved parking for women only near the main entrance.
- For a sauna and work-out, visit My Sportlady Fitness Studio, my-sportlady.de ✉ Klenzestrasse 57b ☎ 20 12 48 🕒 Mon, Wed, Fri 8am–10pm, Tue–Thu 7am–10pm, Sat–Sun 9am–8pm

STUDENT TRAVELERS

- Some museums and theaters offer up to 50 percent discounts with an International Student ID Card.
- A German Rail Youth Pass is available for young people under 26, valid for 3 to 10 days, germanrail-passes.com
- For budget accommodations, camping and youth hostels (▷ 108–9).

Essential Facts

RESTROOMS

Toiletten are marked *Herren* (men) and *Damen* (women). *Besetzt* means occupied, *frei* means vacant. There is often a small charge.

MONEY

The euro is the official currency of Germany. Bank notes are in denominations of €5, €10, €20, €50, €100, €200 and €500 and coins in denominations of 1, 2, 5, 10, 20 and 50 cents and 1 and 2 euros.

ELECTRICITY

● 230 (220–240) volts; two-pin sockets. Take an adaptor with you.

ETIQUETTE

● Say *Grüss Gott* (good day) and *Auf Wiedersehen* (goodbye) when shopping, *Guten Appetit* (enjoy your meal) when eating and *Entschuldigen Sie* (excuse me) in crowds or for minor mishaps.
● Never jump lights at pedestrian crossings. Don't walk on cycle paths.
● Dress is generally informal, except for at the theater, opera or in nightclubs.
● Service is officially included in bills but tipping is customary.

MEDICAL TREATMENT

● A list of English-speaking doctors is available at the British and US consulates.
● Pack enough of any prescription medication you take regularly to last for the duration of your trip.
● Every neighborhood has a 24-hour pharmacy *(Apotheke)*. Look for the address of that night's 24-hour *Apotheke* displayed in the pharmacy windows.
● International pharmacies have staff who speak different languages. Try Bahnhof-Apotheke (Bahnhofplatz 2, tel 5998 9040) or Internationale Ludwigs-Apotheke (Neuhauserstrasse 11, tel 5505 070).

NATIONAL HOLIDAYS

● January 1, January 6, Good Friday, Easter Sunday, Easter Monday, May 1, Ascension Day, Whit Sunday and Whit Monday, Corpus Christi, August 15, October 3, November 1, Day of Repentance and Prayer (during 3rd/4th week in November), Christmas Day, December 26.

NEWSPAPERS AND MAGAZINES

● Bavaria's daily paper, *Süddeutsche Zeitung*, is published in Munich.

- Munich has several local dailies including the *Münchner Abendzeitung*, *tz* and *Bild-Zeitung*.
- The online community forum website toytowngermany.com has a calendar of English-language events in Munich.

OPENING HOURS
- Banks: Monday to Friday 8.30–3.45 (some open Thursday to 5.30, many close 12.30–1.30).
- Shops: Monday to Saturday 9–6 (9–8 in the malls and shopping centers).
- Museums and galleries: Tuesday to Sunday 9 or 10am–5. Some close Monday and public holidays. Many are free on Sunday.

POST OFFICES
- One of the largest post offices is opposite the railway station (Bahnhofplatz 2, tel 0228 5500 5500, open Monday to Friday 6am–8.30pm, Saturday 9–4).
- Most other post offices are open Monday to Friday 8–8, Saturday 9–4.
- Post boxes are bright yellow and clearly marked "Munich" and "other places" *(Andere Orte)*.
- All letters to other countries cost €0.90. There is a single rate for letters and postcards to anywhere in the world.

TELEPHONES
- Munich from abroad: dial 00 49, then the area code 89, followed by the number.
- From Munich: dial 00 and country code (UK 44, Ireland 353, US and Canada 1), then the number.

EMERGENCIES
- Police, tel 110
- Fire tel 112
- Ambulance tel 112
- Dental emergency service tel 723 3093/94
- Poisons emergency service tel 19240
- Rape hotline tel 76 37 37
- Breakdown service tel 01802 22 22 22

LOST PROPERTY
- **Municipal lost property office:**
- ✉ Oetztalerstrasse 17
- 🕐 Mon, Wed, Fri 7.30–12; Tue 8.30–12, 2–6; Thu 8.30–3 ☎ 2 33 960 45
- For anything lost on the urban rail, subway, tram or bus, contact MVV (☎ 0800 344 22 66 00; S-Bahn 1308 6664).
- For items left on Deutsche Bahn trains: **Fundbüro der Bundesbahn**
- ✉ Hauptbahnhof, opposite platform 26 🕐 Mon–Fri 7am–8pm, Sat, Sun, hols 8am–7pm ☎ Hotline 1805 990599

Language

There is one official standard German language, Hochdeutsch (High German), which everyone in the country should be able to understand. However, the regional Bavarian dialect, with a strong local accent, is widely spoken in Munich. The words and phrases that follow are High German.

BASICS

ja	yes
nein	no
bitte	please
danke	thank you
bitte schön	you're welcome
Guten Tag/Grüss Gott	Hello
Guten Morgen	Good morning
Guten Abend	Good evening
Gute Nacht	Good night
Auf Wiedersehen	Goodbye
entschuldigen Sie bitte	excuse me please
sprechen Sie Englisch?	do you speak English?
ich verstehe nicht	I don't understand
Wiederholen Sie das, bitte	Please repeat that
Sprechen Sie langsamer bitte	Please speak more slowly
heute	today
gestern	yesterday
morgen	tomorrow
jetzt	now
gut	good
Ich heisse...	My name is...
Wie heissen Sie?	What's your name?
Ich komme aus...	I'm from...
Wie geht es Ihnen?	How are you?
Sehr gut, danke	Fine, thank you
Wie spät ist es?	What is the time?
wo	where
wann	when
warum	why
wer	who

USEFUL WORDS

klein/gross	small/large
kalt/warm	cold/warm
rechts/links	right/left
geradeaus	straight on
nahe/weit	near/far
geschlossen/offen	closed/open

OUT AND ABOUT	
Wieviel kostet es?	how much does it cost?
teuer	expensive
billig	inexpensive
Wo sind die Toiletten?	Where are the toilets?
Wo ist die Bank?	Where's the bank?
der Bahnhof	station
der Flughafen	airport
das Postamt	post office
die Apotheke	chemist
die Polizei	police
das Krankenhaus	hospital
der Arzt	doctor
Hilfe	help
Haben Sie einen Stadtplan?	Do you have a city map?
Fahren Sie mich bitte zum/zur/nach...	Please take me to...
Ich möchte hier aussteigen	I'd like to get out here
Ich habe mich verlaufen/verfahren	I am lost
Können Sie mir helfen?	Can you help me?

NUMBERS	
eins	1
zwei	2
drei	3
vier	4
fünf	5
sechs	6
sieben	7
acht	8
neun	9
zehn	10
elf	11
zwölf	12
dreizehn	13
zwanzig	20
einundzwanzig	21
dreissig	30
vierzig	40
fünfzig	50
sechszig	60
siebzig	70
achtzig	80
neunzig	90
hundert	100
tausend	1000
million	million

AT THE HOTEL/RESTAURANT	
die Speisekarte	menu
das Frühstück	breakfast
das Mittagessen	lunch
das Abendessen	dinner
der Weisswein	white wine
der Rotwein	red wine
das Bier	beer
das Brot	bread
die Milch	milk
der Zucker	sugar
das Wasser	water
die Rechnung	bill (check)
das Zimmer	room
Ich bin allergisch gegen	I am allergic to
Ich bin Vegetarier	I am a vegetarian

COLORS	
schwarz	black
blau	blue
braun	brown
rot	red
grün	green
weiss	white
gelb	yellow
rosa	pink
orange	orange
grau	grey
lila	purple

Timeline

LUDWIG I, II AND III

Between 1825 and 1848 King Ludwig I transformed Munich into the Athens on the Isar, a flourishing hub of art and learning, and a university city. In 1848 the king abdicated following political unrest and an affair with the dancer Lola Montez.

In 1886 Ludwig II was certified insane and later found mysteriously drowned in the Starnberger See.

King Ludwig III was deposed in 1918 in the Bavarian Revolution, led by Kurt Eisner, Bavaria's first Prime Minister.

777 First recorded mention of Munichen ("the home of the monks").

1158 Henry the Lion founds Munich.

1327 Munich suffers a devastating fire.

1328 Louis IV is made Holy Roman Emperor and Munich becomes temporarily the imperial capital.

1505 Munich becomes the capital of Bavaria.

1634 The plague reduces Munich's population by one third, to 9,000.

1806 Bavaria becomes a kingdom.

1810 A horse race celebrating the marriage of Crown Prince Ludwig starts the tradition of the *Oktoberfest*.

1864 Composer Richard Wagner moves to Munich.

1876 The first trams run in the city.

1900 Munich becomes a focus of the Jugendstil (art nouveau) movement.

1919 The assassination in Munich of Bavaria's first Prime Minister, Kurt Eisner, results in a communist republic.

From left: Jugendstilhaus Ainmillerstrasse; Schloss Linderhof; Schloss Neuschwanstein; tapestry from Neuschwanstein; decoration from the Jugendstilhaus

1933 Hitler comes to power.

1939 World War II commences.

1940 First air attack on Munich.

1945 American troops take Munich.

1946 Munich becomes the capital of the Free State of Bavaria.

1972 A terrorist attack ends the 20th Summer Olympic Games in tragedy.

1980 A bomb attack during the *Oktoberfest* claims 12 lives.

1990 The reunification of Germany.

2003 Munich celebrates 350 years of opera.

2006 Opening ceremony and match of the soccer World Cup in Munich.

2014 As Munich signs up to become a European hydrogen fuel hub, BMW unveils its H2R Hydrogen car.

2018 Munich celebrates its 860th anniversary with a weekend of street parties (June 16–17).

2020 The Allianz Arena in Munich co-hosts the 60th anniversary UEFA European Football Championship.

RICHARD STRAUSS

Munich's greatest composer, Richard Strauss, was born in 1864, and eventually became the city's Kapellmeister (musical director). The breathtaking Bavarian scenery held a magnetic attraction for him, influencing his compositions considerably, and was particularly evident in his *Alpensinfonie*. His operas are still among the world's most popular and a fountain, depicting scenes from *Salome*, stands in the heart of the city as a memorial.

Index

CityPack Munich

Published by AA Publishing, a trading name of AA Media Limited, whose registered office is Fanum House, Basing View, Basingstoke, Hampshire RG21 4EA. Registered number 06112600.

© **AA Media Limited 2018**
First published 1997
New editions 2016 and 2018

Written by Teresa Fisher
Updated by Christopher and Melanie Rice
Series editor Clare Ashton
Design work Tom Whitlock and Liz Baldin
Image retouching and repro Ian Little

Colour separation by AA Digital Department
Printed and bound by Leo Paper Products, China

A CIP catalogue record for this book is available from the British Library.

ISBN 978-0-7495-7978-4

A05593
Maps in this title produced from mapping © MAIRDUMONT / Falk Verlag 2017 and data from openstreetmap.org © OpenStreetMap contributors
Transport map © Communicarta Ltd, UK

The AA would like to thank the following photographers, companies and picture libraries for their assistance in the preparation of this book.

2-18t AA/T Souter; 4tl CL Schmitt/Munich Tourist Office; 5 R Sterflinger/Munich Tourist Office; 6cl AA/C Sawyer; 6c AA/T Souter; 6cr L Kaster/Munich Tourist Office; 6bl R Hetz/ Munich Tourist Office; 6bc AA/T Souter; 6br BBMC Tobias Ranzinger; 7cl AA/M Jourdan; 7c AA/M Jourdan; 7cr AA/M Jourdan; 7bl J Wildgruber/Munich Tourist Office; 7bc AA/M Jourdan; 7br AA Photodisc; 10tr AA/T Souter; 10/11c B Römmelt/Munich Tourist Office; 10/11b AA/C Sawyer; 11tl AA/M Jourdan; 13tl C Reiter/Munich Tourist Office; 13cl AA/T Souter; 13bl AA/T Souter; 14tr AA/M Jourdan; 14cr AA/C Sawyer; 14bcr Bavaria Tourism; 14br AA/M Jourdan; 16tr C Reiter/Munich Tourist Office; 16tcr Bavaria Filmstadt; 16cbr AA/M Jourdan; 17tl AA DigitalVision; 17tcl BBMC Tobias Ranzinger; 17cl AA/M Jourdan; 16/7b B Römmelt/Munich Tourist Office; 18tr AA/C Sawyer; 18tcr AA/T Souter; 18cr Photodisc; 18br A Müller/Munich Tourist Office; 19tl AA/C Sawyer; 19tcl U Romeis/Munich Tourist Office; 19cl H Schmied/Munich Tourist Office; 19bcl H Gebhardt/Munich Tourist Office; 19bl AA/T Souter; 20/21 C Reiter/Munich Tourist Office; 24l AA/M Jourdan; 24tr T Krüger/Munich Tourist Office; 24br AA/M Jourdan; 25t AA/M Jourdan; 25bl AA/C Sawyer; 25br AA/C Sawyer; 26tl AA/T Souter; 26tr AA/T Souter; 27tl A Müller/Munich Tourist Office; 27c AA/C Sawyer; 27tr A Müller/Munich Tourist Office; 28l H Gebhardt/Munich Tourist Office; 28/29t A Müller/Munich Tourist Office; 28/29b B Römmelt/Munich Tourist Office; 28bc S Böttcher/Munich Tourist Office; 29t H Gebhardt/Munich Tourist Office; 29br F Witzig/Munich Tourist Office; 29bc B Römmelt/Munich Tourist Office; 30tl AA/T Souter; 30tr AA/T Souter; 31tl A Müller/Munich Tourist Office; 31tr A Müller/Munich Tourist Office; 32tl PRISMA ARCHIVO / Alamy; 32tr allOver images / Alamy; 33tl B Römmelt/Munich Tourist Office; 33tr C Reiter/Munich Tourist Office; 34-35t AA/M Jourdan; 34bl AA/C Sawyer; 34br C Reiter/Munich Tourist Office; 35 A Müller/Munich Tourist Office; 36 T Krieger/Munich Tourist Office; 37t AA/T Souter; 38t Photodisc; 39t AA/C Sawyer; 40t Digitalvision; 41t AA/M Jourdan; 42t AA/C Sawyer; 43 J Wildgruber/Munich Tourist Office; 46tl Bayerisches Nationalmuseum; 46tc Bayerisches Nationalmuseum; 46tr Bayerisches Nationalmuseum; 47tl AA/T Souter; 47tr BBMC Tobias Ranzinger; 48tl W Hösl/Munich Tourist Office; 48tr U Romeis/Munich Tourist Office; 49tl B Römmelt/Munich Tourist Office; 49tr C Reiter/Munich Tourist Office; 50l W Hösl/Munich Tourist Office; 50tr AA/T Souter; 50br F Mader/Munich Tourist Office; 51t J Lutz/Munich Tourist Office; 51cl AA/T Souter; 51cr AA/M Jourdan; 52-53t AA/M Jourdan; 52bl W Hösl/Munich Tourist Office; 52br AA/C Sawyer; 53b T Krüger/ Munich Tourist Office; 54t AA/T Souter; 55t AA/M Chaplow; 56t Photodisc; 57t W Hösl/ Munich Tourist Office; 58t AA/C Sawyer; 59 J Wildgruber/Munich Tourist Office; 62 © Roy Langstaff / Alamy; 63tl W Hösl/Munich Tourist Office; 63tr AA/C Sawyer; 64l P Scarlandis/ Munich Tourist Office; 64tr H Schmied/Munich Tourist Office; 64c AA/M Jourdan; 65t M Prugger/Munich Tourist Office; 65cl AA/T Souter; 65cr AA/M Jourdan; 66t U Romeis/Munich Tourist Office; 66cl AA/T Souter; 66cr A Müller/Munich Tourist Office; 67tl J Wildgruber/ Munich Tourist Office; 67cl AA/T Souter; 67r AA/T Souter; 68tl C L Schmitt/Munich Tourist Office; 68tr AA/C Sawyer; 69tl J Sauer/Munich Tourist Office; 69tr J Sauer/Munich Tourist Office; 70l G Blank/Munich Tourist Office; 70tr B Römmelt/Munich Tourist Office; 70cr AA/M Jourdan; 71t G Blank/Munich Tourist Office; 71cl AA/M Jourdan; 71cr AA/M Jourdan; 72t AA/M Jourdan; 72bl imageBROKER/Alamy Stock Photo; 72br AA/C Sawyer; 73 AA/T Souter; 74t Photodisc; 75 AA/T Souter; 76t Brand X Pics; 77t AA/M Jourdan; 78 AA/M Jourdan; 79 H Gebhardt/Munich Tourist Office; 82l J Wildgruber/Munich Tourist Office; 82tr Ruggiero/ Munich Tourist Office; 82cr Olympiapark München; 83t H Gebhardt/Munich Tourist Office; 83c Olympiapark München; 84tl AA/M Jourdan; 84tr B Römmelt/Munich Tourist Office; 84cl AA/M Jourdan; 84cr AA/C Sawyer; 85 C Reiter/Munich Tourist Office; 86tl BMW Pictures; 86tr BMW Pictures; 87-88t AA/M Jourdan; 87bl B Römmelt/Munich Tourist Office; 87br B Römmelt/Munich Tourist Office; 88bl AA/T Souter; 88br R Hetz/Munich Tourist Office; 89t AA/T Souter; 90t AA/T Souter; 91t AA/T Souter; 92t AA/M Jourdan; 93 Bavaria Tourism; 96l Bavaria Filmstadt; 97t Bavaria Filmstadt; 97cl Bavaria Filmstadt; 97cr Bavaria Filmstadt; 98l Bavaria Tourism; 98/99t Bavaria Tourism; 98cl Bavaria Tourism; 98c Bavaria Tourism; 98/99 Bavaria Tourism; 99 Bavaria Tourism; 100tl AA/T Souter; 100tr J Wildgruber/Munich Tourist Office; 101-102t AA/M Jourdan; 101bl Allianz Arena/B. Ducke; 101br AA/A Baker; 102b imagebroker/Alamy; 103t-106t Bavaria Tourism; 103b AA/A Baker; 103c AA/T Souter; 103r Bavaria Tourism; 104 AA/A Baker; 105bl Bavaria Tourism; 105bc AA/T Souter; 105br Bavaria Tourism; 106bl AA/T Souter; 106br AA/T Souter; 107 AA/M Jourdan; 108-112t AA/C Sawyer; 108tr Photodisc; 108cr Stockbyte; 108bcr AA/M Jourdan; 108br AA/M Jourdan; 113 robertharding/Alamy; 114-125t J Sauer/Munich Tourist Office; 117b AA/T Souter; 122 AA/T Souter; 124bl AA/C Sawyer; 124bc AA/T Souter; 124br AA/T Souter; 125bl AA/T Souter; 125br AA/C Sawyer

Every effort has been made to trace the copyright holders, and we apologise in advance for any accidental errors. We would be happy to apply the corrections in the following edition of this publication.

Titles in the Series